WHAT IT TAKES TO BE #1

*Vince Lombardi
on Leadership*

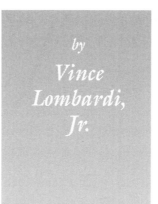

by

Vince
Lombardi,
Jr.

McGRAW-HILL

New York   St. Louis   San Francisco   Washington, D.C.
Auckland   Bogotá   Caracas   Lisbon   London   Madrid
Mexico City   Milan   Montreal   New Delhi   San Juan
Singapore   Sydney   Tokyo   Toronto

Dad,
this is for you

Contents

Acknowledgements

Any important project such as this is a team effort, and a good leader acknowledges everyone who made it possible. So here is a heart-felt thank you to those who made this book a reality. Jill, my wife of thirty-five years, thank you for your patience and understanding. My sons, Vincent, John and Joseph, and especially my daughter, Gina, my computer expert and ever vigilant grammarian. Terry Bledsoe, Ed Cerny and Roger Bel Air, trusted filters for the early version of this work. Jeff Cruikshank, a talent-ed writer, who brought needed organization and clarity to the book. Finally, Jeffrey Krames, McGraw-Hill editor-in-chief and publisher, who exhibited some of Vince Lombardi's "mental toughness" in bringing this effort to successful completion.

Vince Lombardi and the Quest for Leadership

There are no hereditary strata in leading. They're not born; they're made. There has to be an inclination, a commitment, a willingness to command.

Imagine that sometime in the near future you live through one of those opening scenes from *Close Encounters of the Third Kind*.

You're driving your SUV down a deserted country road on a moonlit night. Suddenly, the calm of the summer night is shattered by the arrival of a spaceship, just ahead of you on the road. You are apprehensive, but unafraid. A strange-looking creature emerges, and you discover that you're able to communicate with each other.

The creature looks you in the eye and says,

Take me to your leader.

What will you do? Take him to the White House? To your statehouse? Maybe you'd be more inclined to go roust out the CEO of your company. Maybe the first person you'd think of is your town's mayor or the superintendent of schools.

The creature has asked you to put a face on leadership. For me, and maybe for you, that would be a difficult task today. Why? Because today, a legitimate leader is hard to find. We live in a time when authority is questioned, gratification is instant, morals are relative, ethics are situational, and the truth is apparently what we decide it is. We lead lives of comfort and ease, and as a result, we've lost our hunger to lead and achieve. Today, fewer people are willing to make the sacrifices that are necessary to become a leader.

**Leadership is not just one quality, but rather a
blend of many qualities; and while no one
individual possesses all of the needed talents that**

go into leadership, each man can develop a
combination to make him a leader.

The quote comes from my father, Vince Lombardi. In my opinion, Lombardi developed the qualities and talents that make a leader.

Most people who know football agree. Vince Lombardi was one of the greatest football coaches in the history of the professional game. In 10 seasons as a head coach in the National Football League—9 with the Green Bay Packers and 1 with the Washington Redskins—Lombardi compiled a truly amazing record: 105 wins, 35 losses, and 6 ties.

His Packers played in six World Championship games and won five, including the first two Super Bowls. His postseason record of nine victories and a single defeat is unrivaled in the history of professional football.

So how, exactly, did my father accomplish what he did? How did he attain #1 status? Equally important, how did he consistently *maintain* it?

I believe that the answer to these questions lies not in one game plan or another, but in an approach to life—a philosophy of leadership. And that's what this book is about.

I think I have a unique perspective on Vince Lombardi. He died when I was 28 years old. That means I had the privilege of spending not only my childhood with him, but also much of my young adulthood. As a child, I knew, respected, and loved him, and in those simple times he was simply a father to me. Eventually, I knew that the world saw him as someone special. That only confirmed what the boy already knew.

I also got to know him again as an adult. As I grew older, I came to understand that, just like the rest of us, he had his blind spots and shortcomings. We agreed on the big things, and disagreed on a lot of the smaller ones but I never doubted his leadership abilities. I know I'll never meet another leader quite like him.

A LEADER FOR MANY GENERATIONS

In my own life, I have been a lawyer, politician, writer, and National Football League and United States Football League executive. I've also done a lot of public speaking, and now I do it for a living as a professional speaker. In all of those contexts, I've been amazed at the consistent level of interest that people have shown in my father.

When I speak, I very often have people my own age or older come up to me and tell me that my father was a hero to them. They tell me that they have my father's famous quote, "What It Takes to Be #1," hanging in their office or den. (For more about this, see the last page of this book.) These are people who cut their football teeth on the Packers when the team was at the pinnacle of football success in the 1960s. In addition, the Packers, although from the smallest NFL city, weren't just a local phenomenon. Because of their success, they were very often one of the two teams in the second game of a nationally televised doubleheader, so people from all over the country got to know Vince Lombardi and his proud Packers. In the 1960s, all across America, people grew up on the Packers.

What truly amazes me is the number of younger people, many of them born after my father's death in 1970, who also speak about him as a hero and role model. This is just a guess, but I sometimes think that the level of public interest in my father is actually increasing. (An excellent biography by David Maraniss, published in 1999, has only intensified the spotlight that shines on my father's memory.) How many sports figures are still accumulating new fans 30 years after their death?

What is the cause of this interest—even fascination?

I think people are fascinated by a coach who, although focused and ambitious, wasn't particularly interested in the limelight. (In fact, he was painfully shy, and the kind of easy banter that today's coach is supposed to be able to engage in never came easily to my father.) A coach who didn't land his first head coaching job (other than at the high school level) until the relatively advanced age of

46. A coach who rarely went out of his way to make life easy for journalists and, perhaps because of that, sometimes received rough treatment at their hands.

Obviously, there's a hunger out there for the kind of leadership that my father embodied. I'm not a psychologist nor am I a historian, but it seems to me that a leadership vacuum opened up in this country during the 1960s. Our national leaders looked at the lengthening list of seemingly intractable problems (Vietnam, race relations, and increasing levels of crime and violence) and political humiliations (beginning, but not ending, with Watergate), and a tragic thing happened: *They lost confidence in themselves!*

Then the next tragic thing happened: The rest of us lost confidence in our leaders. In a few short years, we became a nation of doubters, despite the fact that our nation was then (and still is today) the wealthiest, most powerful, and most opportunity-filled nation on earth.

Vince Lombardi was one of the few leaders on the national stage who didn't seem to have any doubts. He was intense. He was articulate. He believed in his leadership ability. And he had a win–loss record that made believers out of a lot of other people. He expressed the opinion, forcefully and unapologetically, that the pursuit of victory—fairly and squarely, and within the rules—was life's great challenge. Not victory for its own sake, but victory as a test— a test of how far you could push yourself to your limits and beyond, a test of your ability to overcome your doubts and weaknesses, and a test of how much of your God-given talent and ability you were willing to expend in the pursuit of success and victory.

A case in point: Vietnam was frustrating in part because it was a limited war. As a nation, how could we commit fully to winning a war that could be fought only in limited ways? And here's someone not from Washington or New York, but from Wisconsin, reminding us what an unlimited commitment looked like. (The similarities between football and warfare probably reinforced this subconscious connection.) Here's someone who, on what seemed like an annual basis, got to celebrate joyful victories. No wonder Vince Lombardi got rooted so deeply in the American psyche!

WHY ANOTHER LEADERSHIP BOOK?

In this book, I want to present a clear picture of my father's leadership model.

I'm sure that there are at least a few people out there who groaned when they read that last sentence: Not another book on leadership! What can possibly be said about leadership that hasn't already been said, ad nauseam?

My answer is, given the absence of leadership today in all walks of life, perhaps a lot has been written about it, but not enough has been read and internalized. How many books and articles about leadership are published every year? Hundreds? Thousands? You'd think that all those authors would have satisfied the demand by now. Not true: In a recent survey of corporate executives in this country, half of the respondents reported that their organizations lack the leadership that will be needed to assure their success into the 21st century.

But I'll be more candid than many authors of leadership books. I'll admit up front that you may not learn anything "new" about leadership from this book. But I think there's an excellent chance that you will find a framework and a model that's compelling, practical, and durable.

In other words, there's a chance that some of the principles outlined in this book will stick with you. And that's the important point. How many diets does it take for you to get down to the weight you want? *Just one:* the one you stick with. How many times do you have to reorganize your desk, your office, your approach to your job before you experience some of the changes you'd like to see? *Just one:* the reorganization you commit to and discipline yourself to stick with. How many different approaches to leadership do you have to sample before you begin to see some positive results? *Just one:* the one that you understand, believe in, internal-ize, commit to, and stick with.

> *Fundamentals win it. Football is two things;*
> *it's blocking and tackling. I don't care about*
> *formations or new defenses or tricks on defense.*
> *If you block and tackle better than the team*
> *you're playing, you'll win.*

Because it is fundamentally sound, I think my father's leadership model was and is a compelling one. It may prove to be the one you can believe in, commit to, and stick with.

Why? In part because leadership is exercised on many levels and in many contexts, and I think my father's model works well on all those levels. It can help you be #1 on the football field (although this is only incidentally a "football book"). It can help you be #1 at the office, in your community, and in the hearts of your loved ones. Lombardi's leadership model is about finishing first, but it's also about finishing what you start, rather than quitting and com-promising on your goals. One of my father's gifts was his ability to turn a few ideas into a call to action:

> *Most important of all, to be successful in life*
> *demands that a man make a personal commitment*
> *to excellence and to victory, even though the*
> *ultimate victory can never be completely won. Yet*
> *that victory might be pursued and wooed with*
> *every fiber of our body, with every bit of our might*
> *and all our effort. And each week, there is a new*
> *encounter; each day, there is a new challenge.*

It's OK with me if somebody says, "This doesn't sound like the model for me." But I hope no one says, "I'm not a leader, so this book isn't for me." Even if you don't sit in the corner office, or give speeches, or lead a pro football franchise, you are a leader or on your way to becoming one. If you're a parent, you're certainly a leader. If you're a good friend or a good neighbor, you're a leader. People are learning from the model of your life. They are deciding to emulate things that you do well—and maybe resolving to avoid doing some of those other things that you do. *You're a leader.* The question is, *What kind of leader are you capable of becoming?*

In this book, I'll draw upon the letters, speeches, and other writings that my father left behind. Unless otherwise attributed, the quotes on these pages are my father's. In his own way, he was an extremely articulate person. I respected that quality in him enormously. So, whenever possible, I'll let him speak for himself.

I'll do my best to quote him in context, protecting the sense of what I think he was trying to say. A lot of my father's comments show up out of context and are confusing, misleading, or both. That's unfortunate. I believe that words have power and energy. As a leader, you can call forth this energy as you link words together. Words are the tools of a leader. (Someone once said that Winston Churchill "mobilized the English language and sent it into battle to steady his fellow countrymen.") In this book, you'll see many examples of how my father used words to persuade people to give him their absolute best effort. You can do the same.

The converse is also true. Used poorly—or maliciously—words can cause great pain and confusion. They can demotivate and negate effort. My father made some mistakes with words, as all leaders do, and we'll look at those as well.

Throughout this book, I'll draw on my personal experiences and understanding of the man. As noted at the beginning of this introduction, I think that my nearly three decades of proximity to him gives me a special insight into his leadership philosophy. Where possible, I'll tease out specific "lessons" that I've learned from my father and set them off from the text for easy reference ("Lombardi's Rules"). Perhaps this tactic will be helpful to the reader; perhaps it won't. The risk is making things too simplistic. But I think people are so busy and so overwhelmed with information today, that they may not have time to dig for buried treasure. I encourage you to pick and choose, and find those things that are useful to you.

I'll also weave my own observations about leadership into the chapters that follow. You should pick and choose among these, too. But as I noted earlier, I've been a manager and a leader in a variety of large and small organizations. I've learned quite a bit about what motivates people and about what works and what doesn't work in a business setting. In the course of my professional speaking career, I've struck up dialogues with literally hundreds of leaders and managers. As a result of the give-and-take in these exchanges, I've absorbed a great deal about the business issues and leadership challenges confronting managers in today's fast-paced workplace.

One last introductory thought: Speaking of those dialogues, I once heard a discussion of a phenomenon called the "tyranny of the or." This "tyranny" would seem to dictate that a leader can be either compassionate "or" results oriented, but not both, fair "or" tough, but not both.

The reality—confirmed by the example of my father—is that a leader can and should possess *all* of these qualities. Indeed, to be a leader, you should possess most or all of the many qualities mentioned in this book. "Balance" is not the answer. In other words, you don't become a leader who is fair by being less firm. You don't become compassionate by being less driven by results. Leaders are fair, disciplined, compassionate, results driven, and all of the other qualities that we will cover in the Lombardi leadership model.

Paradoxical? Yes, but paradox is a universal law. The day you were born is the day you begin to die. Less can be more. Logic and intuition are both necessary qualities for a leader. To lead, you must serve. Leadership cannot be taught, but must be learned. I believe my father was expressing this paradox of leadership when he said,

Leaders no longer understand the relationship between themselves and the people; that is, people want to be independent and dependent, all at the same time, to assert themselves and at the same time be told what to do.

PREVIEW: THE VINCE LOMBARDI LEADERSHIP MODEL

Although he never committed his entire leadership model to paper, my father had some definite ideas on exactly what qualities were required for effective leadership. To Vince Lombardi, traits such as character and integrity were the prerequisites of leadership, and it is these crucial qualities that provide the bedrock for his leadership vision.

Part I of this book, entitled "The Foundation of Leadership," is organized around those vital leadership traits. Part II, "Inspiring Others to Greatness," shows how my father applied those qualities in a leadership setting. Although much more will be said about the model throughout the book (particularly in Chapter 2), I thought it would be helpful to start with a preview of his leadership method. Vince Lombardi felt that leadership was an evolutionary process and that the road to leadership begins with an awareness of oneself. The following flowchart illustrates the evolutionary nature of the leadership process:

Let's briefly look at each element:

Leadership starts with self-knowledge: Self-discovery leads to self-knowledge. Only by knowing yourself—your principles and values—can you hope to become an effective leader.

Self-knowledge is the basis for character: Once you understand yourself, you can start to grow and write your character.

Along with good habits and competence, this creates the skills required for effective leadership.

Character is the root of integrity: Without character, asserts Vince Lombardi, there can be no integrity.

Integrity provides the foundation of leadership: Character and integrity are the two pillars of effective leadership.

ॐ

I hope that this book helps you become the leader you aspire to be and makes your victories come sooner and your successes more meaningful and enduring.

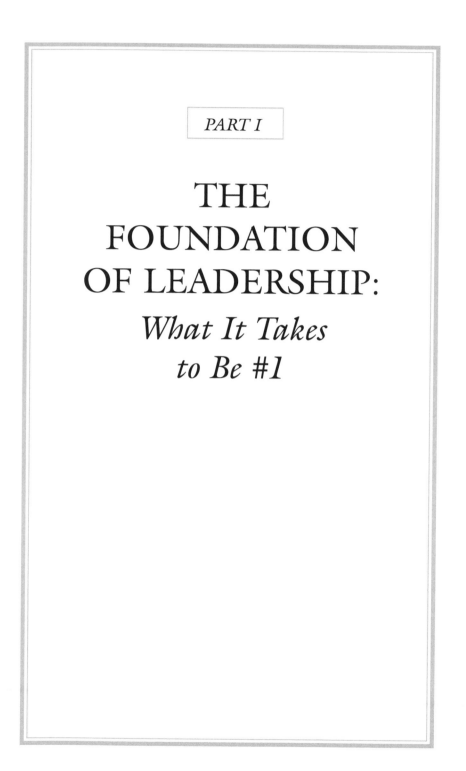

PART I

THE FOUNDATION OF LEADERSHIP:

What It Takes to Be #1

Chapter 1

Lombardi on Lombardi

I've been in football all my life, gentlemen, and I don't know whether I'm particularly qualified to be a part of anything else, except I consider it a great game, a game of many assets, by the way, and I think a symbol of what this country's best attributes are: courage and stamina and a coordinated efficiency or teamwork.

At many a moment on many a day, I am convinced that pro football must be a game for madmen, and I must be one of them.

I s it possible for one person to label a game—professional football—both a symbol of this country's best attributes and a game for madmen?

Is it possible for one person to be shy, cautious, moody, short tempered, autocratic, demanding, confident, friendly, warm, and considerate?

Is it possible for a single person to evoke the emotions of awe, affection, hate, fear, and respect in the people around him?

Sure, it is. I have known one such person: my father, Vince Lombardi. He had all those qualities. He inspired all those reactions in the many people whose lives he touched. Without ever trying to be complicated or sophisticated, he was that paradox we just talked about in the prologue.

In this chapter, I want to introduce my father to people who never knew him. Throughout the book, I'll make references to episodes from the major phases of his life, so it seems sensible to include a brief biographical sketch for the benefit of those people who have only a vague idea of who "Vince Lombardi" was and why we're still talking about him 30 years after his passing. But let me emphasize that this is not a biography of my father. For those in search of a comprehensive and chronological picture of his life, two excellent biographies already are out there (*Vince*, by Michael O'Brien, and David Maraniss' *When Pride Still Mattered*, mentioned in the prologue), as are a number of more focused books, including a lively and insightful write-up of his year with the

Redskins (*Coach*, by Tom Dowling) and my father's own *Run to Daylight*.

And since much of this book is going to consist of my own reflections on my father's leadership model, as well as my own experiences as a leader, I'll begin this chapter with a couple of selected stories that illustrate the complex, difficult, intense, and rewarding relationship that existed for almost three decades between two guys named Vince Lombardi: father and son.

GROWING UP LOMBARDI

My relationship with my father was probably a lot like that of other people who spent any amount of time with Vince Lombardi— although, in my case, a bit more intense. The feelings generated within those relationships covered the emotional spectrum, ranging from respect and love on the one hand to intense dislike on the other. And with my father, you could walk that entire spectrum in the course of a five-minute conversation.

I recall vividly an episode that occurred when I was a freshman at the then-College (now University) of St. Thomas in St. Paul, Minnesota. I had gone to school early for football practice, but I had hurt my knee and wasn't playing. This was frustrating for me. It was mid-September, the season was underway, and I wanted to be out there practicing with my teammates.

One of those September weekends, the Green Bay Packers, with Coach Lombardi, came to Minneapolis to play the Vikings. I had spent my summers over the last few years doing chores at the Packer training camps, and I had stood on the sidelines at dozens of Packer games, watching the team earn its reputation as the best in pro football. I knew many of the players well, and some I considered my friends. So I looked forward to seeing them again, as I limped into the lobby of the hotel where they were staying. I wasn't disappointed. A group of Packers who were waiting to check in greeted me warmly and gave me all kinds of sympathy for my injured knee.

Then I went up to my father's suite. He welcomed me with a big bear hug and one of his huge smiles. I basked in the warmth of his affection. There was nothing quite like the feeling you got when Vince Lombardi made you feel welcome.

My father knew about my knee, so he arranged to have Dr. Jim Nellen, the team physician, take a look at me. Nellen turned my leg this way and that, pushed and probed with his fingers, and said that although the joint was a little loose, there was nothing else wrong with my knee.

Upon hearing this, my father lit into me. He yelled at me in no uncertain terms to *quit babying that knee and start running on it.* I was hurt, embarrassed, and reduced to tears. From loving father to demanding taskmaster, in a matter of minutes!

But it wouldn't be fair to end the anecdote there. It turns out that my father made the right call. I ran on the knee the next day, and it didn't feel as bad as I thought it would. I started my first varsity game a couple of weeks later, well ahead of my expected recovery schedule.

The Good Lord gave you a body that can stand most anything. It's your mind you have to convince.

A second story: At the end of my freshman year at St. Thomas, I made a dumb mistake. Caught up in the pressures and anxieties of final exams, I forgot to arrange for on-campus housing for the following fall. When I got back to school at the end of that summer for football practice, I discovered that I had no place to live.

Well, no big deal. I got together with four of my teammates, and we rented the top floor of a house a few blocks from campus. To the extent that I thought about it at all, I guess I thought that I had come up with a good solution to a problem that should never have come up in the first place. I happened to mention the solution to my mother the next time I called home.

Bright and early the next morning, my father called the dean of students. "Send my son home," he told the dean in a non-negotiable tone of voice. "He's not living off campus." Or that's what the dean told me when I was called in to get the news. Again, I was angry and embarrassed, but my father's word was law. The school found me a room on campus, and I moved out of my "bachelor pad," leaving my teammates behind.

And once again, that's not quite the end of the story. Without the temptations of off-campus living to deal with, I made the dean's list both semesters that year. Meanwhile, of the four guys I had originally arranged to live with, two were back on campus by the second semester, another took six years to graduate, and the last never did graduate. My father, it turned out, knew me better than I knew myself—or, at least, he was able to make a good guess about the pitfalls that might await me if I set up housekeeping with four other sophomores.

Before I can embrace freedom, I should be aware of what duties I have.

Flash forward to about six years later, when I was 26 years old and married with a couple of kids. My wife, Jill, and I traveled to Milwaukee for a Packer pre-season game. As I recall it, I hadn't seen my parents for about six months, and in the interim, I had grown my sideburns pretty long. This was the late '60s, and most males my age had at least a little extra hair on their faces.

I walk into my parents' room—a certified adult, two kids!—and my father barks out, "Get rid of those sideburns!" So I turn around, go back to my room, and shave my sideburns.

Some disputes between my father and me weren't resolved quite so quickly. During my senior year in high school, I mentioned to him that I thought that I'd major in physical education at college because I wanted to be a coach. He fixed his intense stare on me for a few seconds. "That's OK," he said curtly, "but if you do, I'll not put one penny toward your education."

Needless to say, that got my attention. "Well," I asked, "what do you think I should do?"

"I think you should go to law school."

"I'm not going to law school!"

So began a debate that went on for four full years. When I got to be a senior, I realized I had nothing better to do, so I applied to law school, got accepted to the University of Minnesota, and enrolled there. Within a few short weeks, I quit. I decided that I had been right all along: I didn't want to go to law school. My father was very disappointed in me, and in his own way he let me know about it. At the time, I decided it wouldn't be prudent to point out to him that he had done more or less the same thing, dropping out of Fordham Law School after an unhappy year there.

Time passed. I got married, started getting serious about a family and other adult responsibilities, and realized that I needed more education. So I went back to law school at night. This was a terrible grind. Jill deserves enormous credit for holding our marriage and our family together during those four years when I worked days, went to school at nights, and generally was an absent partner and parent.

But what do I remember best about that difficult period? I remember the enormous pride that my father felt in me on that hot June night when I finally graduated from William Mitchell College of Law. "My son, the *lawyer*," he said to everyone within earshot, grinning that famous grin.

> *I tend to believe in catching stars, and have been*
> *willing to take my chances on the hernia.*

Recently, somebody tried to tell me that I had been abused as a child. I thought about that for about two seconds and decided that it was nonsense. When I did something wrong, breaking a rule of the household, I was punished. Punishment could take the form of a firm whack on some part of my anatomy, or banishment to my room, or being assigned some particularly dirty job.

Needless to say, I didn't like getting punished. But you know what? It worked. Pretty soon, I began to make the all-important connection of cause and effect: *You screw up; you pay the conse-quences.* I think this was a very valuable lesson, and it's one that fewer and fewer parents seem to be teaching today. I never felt that I was a victim. Instead, I reached the conclusion that there were people out there—starting with my father and mother, Marie— who deserved my respect. And when I gave them their due respect, I started earning their respect back. That's what a lot of my own struggles with my father were all about.

> *Don't succumb to excuses. Go back to the job of making the corrections and forming the habits that will make your goal possible.*

A WINNER'S CAREER IN FOOTBALL

Let's briefly review my father's background and career to see how he formed his leadership habits. Vincent Thomas Lombardi was born on June 11, 1913, to a vibrant and sprawling Italian-American family living in Sheepshead Bay, New York. That neighborhood was a section of Brooklyn that had once been an upper class summer resort area, but had gradually been transformed into a community for the immigrants pouring into the city through Ellis Island. His father and uncle ran Lombardi Bros., a meat wholesaler, and young Vince got his first business education from his father, who, although more or less unschooled, ran a successful business in a cutthroat industry and an unforgiving city.

When he was 15, Lombardi enrolled at Cathedral Prep, a school run by the Brooklyn diocese for Catholic boys who hoped to become priests. Although Lombardi ultimately left Cathedral and chose a different path for himself, the Church remained a central part of his belief system and his daily ritual for the rest of his life.

But the reason he left Cathedral was his other great passion: football. The priests who ran the school strongly disapproved of football, which they condemned as violent. Vince switched to St.

Francis Prep, Brooklyn's oldest Catholic school, where he was able to play competitive football for the first time. He reached his adult height and weight as a teenager, so he could hold his own physically. But more important, he discovered an *intensity* about football that almost guaranteed that he would play while more talented athletes with less drive stayed on the bench.

Brains without competitive hearts are rudderless.

Lombardi enrolled at Fordham University in the fall of 1933, football scholarship in hand. Fordham was a cloistered, intense environment, run by members of the intellectually rigorous Jesuit order. The priests pushed him hard, perhaps for the first time in his life, to think about the world and his place within it. The Jesuits believed that humans could perfect themselves through hard work and dedication to excellence, principles that guided Lombardi for the rest of his life.

Meanwhile, Fordham's football coach, Jim Crowley—made legendary years earlier by sportswriter Grantland Rice as one of Notre Dame's "Four Horsemen"—pushed Vince as a football player. As it turned out, Lombardi was both injury-prone and not a particularly gifted athlete. But Fordham had good teams in the mid-1930s, and the defensive line (including an intense guard named Butch Lombardi) achieved regional celebrity as the "Seven Blocks of Granite" that refused to yield to its opponents.

After college, my father cast about for a purpose in life for two years. He didn't want to work in the family meat business. He enrolled in Fordham Law School (his father's idea!), but abandoned that effort after a year. Finally, in the fall of 1939, he took a job at St. Cecilia, a parochial school in Englewood, New Jersey, where a Fordham classmate hired him as an assistant football coach. It wasn't a full-time job, of course: Lombardi was also expected to teach physics, chemistry, and Latin. My father wooed and won his girlfriend, Marie Planitz—whose conservative

Irish–German family wasn't so sure about an Italian son-in-law—
and the building blocks of his adult life were now all in place: religion, family, and football.

I was born on April 27, 1942. There was apparently some confusion about whether I was to be named "Vincent Thomas Lombardi,
Jr." My father seems to have insisted that I take his father's first name,
Henry, as my middle name. My mother agreed, and I, of course, had
no opinion on the subject. So I'm not a "Jr.," although I've usually
gone by that name simply because it avoids a lot of confusion.

That was the same year that my father became head coach at
"Saints" (as it was known locally) and began to build a local reputation as a football coach. At one point, Saints ran off a string of
32 unbeaten games, an astounding accomplishment for a relatively small parochial school. Lombardi parlayed this success into an
assistant coaching position at his alma mater, Fordham, which he
took up in the summer of 1947. (This was a few months after my
sister, Susan, was born, rounding out our family.) Two years later,
in January 1949, he took yet another assistant position, this time
at the United States Military Academy at West Point, where he
worked for head coach Colonel Earl H. "Red" Blaik.

Blaik was yet another formative influence on Lombardi. Blaik
was devoted to football; it was more or less his entire life. He loved
studying films of games, a relatively unknown technique back in
the late 1940s, and worked his coaches and his players hard. He
was both rigid and flexible, and he had a gift for making complex
things simple, traits my father successfully imitated. Blaik also was
a personal friend of General Douglas MacArthur, and my father
was sometimes assigned the task of showing Army game films from
the preceding Saturday to the aging general in his eagle's nest atop
New York's Waldorf-Astoria Towers.

In 1954, my father broke into the professional ranks when he took
a job as an assistant coach for the New York Giants. He had hopes
of getting the Giants' head coaching job, but wound up as the

offensive assistant to Jim Lee Howell. By this time, Lombardi felt that he had a lot to contribute to a football team's success, and at the Giants' summer training camp in 1954 he introduced his ideas to some skeptical pros. Eventually, both sides met in the middle, for the benefit of all. Lombardi learned how to work with very gifted professional athletes, and the athletes were reintroduced to discipline and hard work.

Howell had the benefit of two extraordinary assistants: my father on offense and player–coach Tom Landry on defense. Both went on to lead professional teams to great successes—my father at Green Bay and Landry at Dallas. They turned the Giants into winners, and other teams took notice. In 1957, the Philadelphia Eagles asked my father to take their head coaching position. It was tempting: After all, there were only 12 such jobs in the world, and the other 11 were spoken for. But the Eagles were in disarray not only on the field, but off the field as well. After much agonizing, he turned the Eagles down, hoping for an opportunity with a team with a better management structure.

That opportunity came at the end of 1958, when one of the worst franchises in the NFL, the lowly Green Bay Packers, asked Lombardi to take over as their head coach. The once-proud Packers had just finished a miserable 1–10–1 season, the worst in the team's history. Lombardi knew he was in a strong bargaining position, and he took full advantage of that knowledge. He signed on as coach and general manager, which effectively gave him complete operating control over the team.

Most people with any knowledge of football know what happened over the course of the next decade, and I've already mentioned those remarkable events in the introduction to this book. I'll have a lot to say in subsequent chapters about how Lombardi accomplished these feats and what leadership lessons we should draw from those accomplishments.

ॐ

My father's professional life was devoted mainly to making his teams successful. (He didn't tolerate outside interests interfering with his players' dedication to their game and certainly wouldn't have put himself in that situation.) So when I refer to my father as a leader, a manager, and a businessperson, I'm referring mainly to his experience as a football coach and executive.

As the Packers' general manager, Lombardi ran a tight ship, and he ran it conservatively. He effectively dominated the Packers' seven-person executive board, a result of his success on the field, his generally recognized insight into people, and his forceful personality. (He could be a hard man to argue with.) In addition, though, the board gave Lombardi a lot of latitude in part because he and its members were philosophically in tune. My father's reluctance to award big contracts, for example, dovetailed neatly with the board's own fiscal conservatism.

I was a fly on the wall for most of those years in Green Bay, and I got the opportunity to see how my father ran his organization. He was an effective delegator, especially—as we'll see in Chapter 7—when it came to things not directly related to the success of the team on the field. He found ways to compensate in areas where he didn't have much experience, especially at the outset of his professional coaching career. He didn't hesitate to ask questions when he didn't understand something, and he didn't tolerate answers that he considered half-baked.

Some front-office workers never stopped seeing him as intimidating and authoritarian. But others realized that he welcomed respectful challenges, especially when someone could make a strong case that he was wrong.

> *You can call me a dictator. The fact is that I am reluctant to take any step that doesn't have the wholehearted support of my whole staff.*

He hated wasting time. He ran tight, agenda-driven meetings that began—and ended—on schedule. Meetings focused on exchanging information and decisions, and decisions were final.

*A meeting is only a means of communication. Its
purpose should be to produce a change in
procedure. This procedure could be in knowledge,
attitude, behavior, or skill. In our meetings,
management gives information, it collects
information, it pools information, and it discusses
the best way to approach the problem. We have
one hard and fast rule: Once the group is agreed
upon the method, there is no deviation until the
group agrees to the change.*

In other words, no second-guessing and no backbiting, a policy
that fostered solidarity and loyalty among his assistants. He further
earned the loyalty of those assistants by paying them well and using
their time wisely. And, of course, everybody loved being associated
with a *winner.*

In the years that he served the Packers as coach and general
manager, he limited his outside activities mainly to the occasional
product endorsement and speaking engagement. (The number of
opportunities to do both, of course, went up sharply as the
Packers crept into the national consciousness as winners.) At first,
he spoke primarily to local groups, but as he became a national
figure, he spoke to groups across the country. At first, he favored
gatherings at which he felt some natural kinship with the people—
such as Catholic charitable events—but over time he accepted
more offers to speak to organizations like the National Association
of Manufacturers (NAM) and other industry groups. His themes
remained consistent, even as his platform got bigger. The advice
he gave to the fund-raisers at St. Elizabeth's Hospital in Appleton,
Wisconsin, in 1962 could have been replayed years later at the
NAM convention:

*In order to succeed, this group will need a
singleness of purpose, they will need a dedication,*

*and they will have to convince all of their
prospects of the willingness to sacrifice.*

For most of his career, my father didn't get involved in any other
outside activities. One exception came in 1968. He was persuaded
to play himself in a motivational sales training film distributed by a
Chicago-based company. I'll cite his comments from that film at
various points in this book, since it presented a pretty concise summary of his leadership model. Called *Second Effort*, the film showed
an earnest, but hapless, salesman being shown the ropes by Coach
Lombardi. The plot was almost nonexistent, and the acting was
pretty amateurish. (I told my father that he was no threat to Richard
Burton or Paul Newman; in response, he demanded to know what
he should have done differently to turn in a better performance.)

But any weaknesses in the acting or the story line turned out to
be unimportant: The film was a runaway success. It sold 10 times
more copies than most films of its type—more than 8,000 units—
and earned my father a significant amount of money in royalties.
"Not bad for four days' work" I heard him chuckle on more than
onc occasion. The film is still in demand today, and I have the roy-
alty checks to prove it.

ℬ

He stepped down as Packer head coach at the end of the 1967 season, retaining his general manager's job. Although he needed a
break and a change, he realized quickly that he had made a serious
mistake. After a year of self-imposed idleness, he surprised the football world by announcing that he had agreed to serve as the head
coach of the Washington Redskins, a team run by the celebrated
lawyer Edward Bennett Williams.

We're going to have a winner the first year.

He was putting the "Lombardi Legend" on the line. He had
never had a losing season as a professional coach. The Redskins were

an average team, playing .500 ball for a dozen years, and they had not won a championship for almost 30 years. Once again, as he had a decade earlier in Green Bay, Lombardi turned things around, mostly through the force of his own personality and through the heroic efforts of a small group of talented Redskin players who understood and bought into the Lombardi vision. Together, they led the team to a respectable 7–5–2 record in the 1969 season.

As it turned out, it was my father's last season. He was taken ill in the spring of 1970 and hospitalized in June with intestinal distress. The grim diagnosis: a virulent cancer of the colon. He died on September 3, 1970, and the football world—and a good piece of the larger world as well—felt the loss.

LOMBARDI AS LEGEND

When he held his first news conference in Washington as the newly appointed head coach of the Redskins, there was considerable excitement in the nation's capital. The Redskins were not quite as hapless as the Packers had been 10 years earlier—but they desperately needed help. And by all accounts, Lombardi was the man to give it to them. "In Green Bay," as one sportswriter reminded the world at that time, "he was widely known as St. Vincent."

What would Lombardi tell the 100-or-so journalists who had assembled to hear his maiden D.C. press conference? "Gentlemen," he began, "it is not true that I can walk across the Potomac River—not even when it is frozen."

When a group of old friends in Bergen County, New Jersey, began trying to arrange a "Vince Lombardi Day," they sought his counsel. "I don't think Vince Lombardi is important enough to have a day set aside for him," my father wrote to the group, in a gentle effort to head off the event.

Being considered a living legend was "embarrassing as the devil," he told a *Sports Illustrated* writer. "Nobody wants to be a legend, really," he told another writer.

Well, I knew my father pretty well, and I think he actually had mixed feelings on the subject of being a legend. He enjoyed mixing with presidents and corporate leaders; he savored the opportunities that his belated fame had afforded him. He loved being associated with a hugely successful franchise and was willing to accept his share of the credit for that success. He had no fear of being "found out" and being revealed as a fraud, as so many celebrities later confess to having felt when they first achieved success. He knew he was good. There was nothing to find out.

"I'm wrong just about as often as I'm right," he wrote modestly of himself. Sometimes he stressed how important luck was, in the era of parity in professional football. "Like a golfer who remembers each shot," recalled the late Steelers owner Art Rooney, "Lombardi remembered all the breaks of the season that went in his favor, fumbles recovered, punts that rolled out of bounds instead of into the end zone."

Again, I take all this with a grain of salt. He never talked about luck with his players; he talked about *preparation*. And on more than one occasion, he used the parity argument to make exactly the opposite point: Luck doesn't favor the lucky; it favors the prepared team. "In pro football," he once told an assistant, "the balance of personnel is so even that the difference between success and failure is player control—in every phase."

So again, we have a paradoxical, somewhat elusive figure at the heart of this book. My father made forceful statements—statements that he obviously believed—that were contradictory. He sometimes said less than he intended to say and puzzled his listeners. He sometimes said more than he intended to say and had to beat a quick retreat. For all of these reasons, we will have to proceed carefully as we attempt to tease his leadership model out of the things he said and did.

Red Blaik, the head coach at West Point who taught Lombardi much of what he knew about coaching football, once made an ear-grabbing statement about my father: "Lombardi," Blaik said, "is a thoroughbred with a vile temper."

Looking through some of my father's papers after his death, I found some more observations by Blaik. In May 1966, Fordham University honored Vince Lombardi with its *Insignis* Medal, an award that my father found enormously gratifying. The speaker who introduced my father that night was "Red" Blaik. His comments, which follow in their entirety, set up much of the discussion that will follow in later chapters:

> He is volatile, and of a temper which he controls like a thermostat.
> But he is also mellow and rich with affection that he shares with
> players, friends, and even at rare times with rivals.

> He is a demanding fundamentalist, intolerant of those who
> fail to meet their own potential. But he is also a tireless teacher
> who respects the intellect and spares no effort to make a depressed
> [Bart] Starr into the great quarterback he is.

> He is motivated to success—to win, if you will—not for
> personal glory but rather for the personal satisfaction that
> comes from great accomplishment.

> He is strong willed and on occasion tactless,
> but never one to state that he "was misquoted."

> He is capable of warm fellowship, but believes strongly that respect is
> the essential ingredient that cements successful human relations.

> He is fearless and of great candor, but he also knows it takes
> a special emotional and mental drive to overcome the personal
> fallibility that one knows who must make the great decision.

> And with it all, he is strictly a human guy, with an infectious
> personality—moody on occasion, but always buoyed by
> proud family ties, unfailing dedication to his friends,
> to his church, and to his high principles.

I think this is an apt description of a reluctant legend—and more important, a leader.

Chapter 2

The Vince Lombardi Leadership Model

Management is leadership. When management fails, it reflects a lack of leadership. All of you possess leadership ability. But leadership rests not only on outstanding ability. It also rests on commitment, loyalty, and pride. It rests on followers who are ready to accept guidance. Leadership is the ability to direct people and—more important—to have those people accept that direction.

At some point in the mid-1960s, my father began giving what I will call "The Speech."

I have a red file folder full of variations on The Speech. They are far more alike than they are different from each other. Of course, my father would tailor the beginning and end of The Speech and sometimes insert some appropriate jokes and anecdotes, to make The Speech more relevant to a specific audience. But the core of The Speech was more or less unchanged, from banquet hall to convention center to college auditorium.

In the late 1960s, when social unrest was on the rise, he modified The Speech considerably, doubling its length and giving it a more overtly political cast. But all of the basic building blocks from the original version of The Speech were carried forward.

All told, he must have given a version of The Speech hundreds of times. (My mother used to say, half in jest, that she had heard it *thousands* of times.) In less formal settings, he would work from a half-dozen five-inch-square photocopied sheets, with a combination of typed and written code phrases that moved him through the body of The Speech ("Ldrs lonely people—cordial, remote, maintain distance himself & group"). In speeches to large groups, he usually had a typed-out version of The Speech, on which he might make notes in advance.

In all cases, he felt free to improvise, and he often did improvise, usually elaborating on his tried-and-true themes. This is another reason there are variations upon variations of The Speech.

This chapter begins with a representative version of The Speech, which I've put together from the many versions in my file. (I'll leave out the "political modules" that Lombardi inserted toward the end of his life, since these are somewhat dated and don't bear directly on the main themes of this book anyway.) I'll use the title my father most often used—"Leadership"—since that was so much his passion and is the focus of this book.

THE SPEECH

As we'll see, The Speech contains the core of what I'll call "the Lombardi leadership model." In the second half of the chapter, I'll present the essentials of that model, which serves as the framework for several of the chapters that follow.

LEADERSHIP

A year ago, in making a talk to a similar group in a similar situation, I had a difficult time in arriving at a method of approach: how to reach this intelligent audience?

Then, finally, I arrived at the only subject through which I could conceivably contribute anything—my own experience of trampling grapes in my local vineyard—namely, football.

I have been in football all my life, and I do not know whether I am particularly qualified to do much else except coach football. I can only say it is a great game, a game of great lessons, a game that has become a symbol of this country's best attributes—namely, courage, stamina, and coordinated efficiency.

It is a Spartan game, and requires Spartan-like qualities in order to play it. By that, of course, I don't mean the Spartan tradition of leaving the weak to die. I mean, instead, the qualities of sacrifice, self-denial, dedication, and fearlessness.

Football is a violent game. To play it any other way but violently would be imbecilic. But because of its violent nature, it demands a personal discipline seldom found in modern life.

Football is more than the National Football League alone. Football is Red Grange, Jim Thorpe, and the many hundreds of other stars who have made this the great game that it is. Football is all of the thousands of high school and college boys who play it and the many millions more who watch it, either in person or on television.

Regardless of what level it is played upon—high school, college, or the professional level—it has become a game that not only exemplifies this country's finest attributes, but more than that, it has the means and the power to provide mental and physical relaxation to the millions who watch it from the sidelines.

I need no other authority than the great General MacArthur to prove my point, and I quote him:

> *Competitive sports keeps alive in all of us a spirit of vitality and enterprise. It teaches the strong to know when they are weak, and the brave to face themselves when they are afraid. It teaches us to be proud and unbending in defeat, yet humble and gentle in victory. It teaches us to master ourselves before we attempt to master others. It teaches us to learn to laugh, yet never forget how to weep. It gives a predominance of courage over timidity.*

I sometimes wonder whether those of us who love football fully appreciate its great lessons. For example: that it is a game played by more than a million Americans and yet, a game uninhibited by racial or social barriers.

It is a game that requires, in early season, exhaustive hard work to the point of drudgery. A game of team action, wherein the individual's reward is that total satisfaction that is returned by being part of the successful whole. A game that gives you 100-percent fun when you win and exacts 100-percent resolution when you lose.

A game like war and also a game most like life—for it teaches that work, sacrifice, perseverance, competitive drive, selflessness, and respect for authority are the price one pays to achieve worthwhile goals.

And it has larger implications. Today, all of us are engaged in a struggle more fiercely contested and far more important to our future. It is the struggle for the hearts, the minds, and the souls of men. In this struggle, there are no spectators, only players. It is a struggle that will test our courage, our strength, and our stamina. Only if we are physically, mentally, and spiritually fit will we win.

We live in an age fit for heroes. No time has ever offered such perils or such prizes. Man can provide a full life for humanity—or he can destroy himself with the problems he has created. The test of this century will be whether man confuses the growth of wealth and power with the growth of spirit and character. If he does, he will be like some infant playing with matches who destroys the very house he would have inherited.

You are the leaders of this country. I believe it is the obligation of our leaders to see that we are awakened to this need. Unless we can do something to get everyone in America moving in this direction, we may not be able to keep America strong.

Calisthenics, exercise, and muscle toning are not the complete answer. There is also a need to develop a strong spirit of competitive interest throughout the nation. In other words, a strong body is only one-half of the answer. We fail in our obligation if we do not also preserve the American zeal to be first and the will to win.

American freedom—and I mean freedom, not license—could be lost and possibly succumb to the consequence of aggressive secularism and communism, unless the values underlying that freedom are thoroughly understood and embraced by our leaders.

For decades, we as individuals have struggled to liberate ourselves from ancient tradition, congealed creeds, and despotic states. In this struggle, freedom was necessarily idealized against order, the new against the old, and genius against discipline. Everything was done to strengthen the right of the individual and weaken the authority of the state and church.

Maybe the battle was too completely won. Maybe we have too much freedom. Maybe we have so long ridiculed authority in the family, discipline in education, decency in conduct, and law in the state that our freedom has brought us close to chaos.

Maybe our leaders no longer understand the relationship between themselves and the people—that is, that the people want to be independent and dependent, all at the same time. They want to assert themselves and yet at the same time be told what to do.

Management *is* leadership. When management fails, it reflects a lack of leadership. All of you possess leadership ability. But leadership rests not only on outstanding ability. It also rests on commitment, loyalty, and pride. It rests on followers who are ready to accept guidance. Leadership is the ability to direct people and—more important—to have those people accept that direction.

The educated man is the natural leader. He may not get all of his education in college; in fact, his inspiration may come from anyplace. If he studies the past, his country, his people, his ancestry, and the lessons of history, he is educated.

I think you will agree that what is needed in the world today is not just engineers and scientists. What is needed, too, is people who will keep their heads in an emergency, no matter what the field. Leaders, in other words, who can meet intricate problems with wisdom and with courage.

Leadership is not just one quality, but rather a blend of many qualities. And while no one individual possesses all of the talents that are needed for leadership, each man can develop a combination that can make him a leader. Contrary to the opinion of many, leaders are not born; they are made. And they are made by hard effort, which is the price we must all pay for success.

We are not born equal. Rather, we are born unequal. The talented are no more responsible for their talent than the underprivileged are for their position. The measure of each is what he does.

Our society, at the present time, seems to have sympathy only for the misfit, the ne'er-do-well, the maladjusted, the criminal, the loser. It is time to stand up for the doer, the achiever, the one who sets out to do something and does it. The one who recognizes the problems and opportunities at hand, and deals with them, and is successful, and is not worrying about the failings of others. The one who is constantly looking for more to do. The one who carries the work of the world on his shoulders. The leader. We will never create a good society, much less a great one, until individual excellence is respected and encouraged.

To be a leader, you must be honest with yourself. You must know that as a leader, you are "like everyone else"—only more so. You must identify yourself with the group and back them up, even at the risk of displeasing your superiors. You must believe that the group wants, above all else, the leader's approval. Once this feeling prevails, productivity, discipline, and morale will all be high. In return, you must demand from the group cooperation to promote the goals of the corporation.

As a leader, you must believe in teamwork through participation. As a result, your contacts with the group must be close and informal. You must be sensitive to the emotional needs and expectations of others. In return, the group's attitude toward the leader should be one of confidence infused with affection.

And yet, the leader must always walk the tightrope between the consent he must win and the control he must exert. Despite the need for teamwork and participation, the leader can never close the gap between himself and the group. If he does, he is no longer what he has to be. The leader is a lonely person. He must maintain a certain distance between himself and the members of the group.

A leader does not exist in the abstract, but rather in terms of what he does in a specific situation. A leader is judged in terms of what others do to obtain the results that he is placed there to get.

You, as a leader, must possess the quality of mental toughness. This is a difficult quality to explain, but in my opinion, this is the most important element in the character of the leader.

Mental toughness is many things. It is humility. It is simplicity. The leader always remembers that simplicity is the sign of true greatness and meekness, the sign of true strength. Mental toughness is Spartanism, with all its qualities of self-denial, sacrifice, dedication, fearlessness, and love.

Yes, love. "Love" is not necessarily "liking." You do not need to like someone in order to love them. Love is loyalty. Love is teamwork. Love is respect for the dignity of an individual. Love is charity. The love I speak of is not detraction. A man who belittles another—who is not loyal, who speaks ill of another—is not a leader and does not belong in the top echelons of management.

I'm not advocating that love is the answer to everything. I am not advocating a love that forces everyone to love everybody else. I am not saying that we must love the white man because he is white, or the black man because he is black, or the poor man because he is poor, or the enemy because he is the enemy, or the perverse because he is perverse. Rather, I am advocating a love for the human being—any human being, who just happens to be white, black, poor or rich, enemy or friend.

Heart power is the strength of your company, of your organization, of America. Hate power is the weakness of the world.

Mental toughness is also the perfectly disciplined will. The strength of your group is in your will—in the will of the leader. The difference between a successful man and others is not in the lack of strength, nor in the lack of knowledge, but rather, in the lack of will. The real difference between men is in energy. It is in the strong will, the settled purpose, the invincible determination.

But remember that the will is the character in action. If we would create something, we must be something. This is character. Character is higher than intellect. Character is the direct result of mental attitude. A man cannot dream himself into character; he must hammer and forge one for himself. He cannot copy someone else's qualities; he must develop his own character qualities to fit his own personality.

> We should remember, too, that there is only one kind of discipline, and that is the perfect discipline. As a leader, you must enforce and maintain that discipline; otherwise, you will fail at your job.
> Leadership lies in sacrifice, self-denial, love, fearlessness, and humility.
> And this is the distinction between great and little men.

So that's a version of The Speech. It was last delivered in Dayton, Ohio, on June 22, 1970. A week later, my father entered a hospital in Washington, D.C., for treatment of excruciating stomach pains. He died three months later.

Why should we pay attention to a speech that hasn't been heard in 30 years? I think there are a couple of reasons.

First, there is a continuing fascination with Lombardi's life and the philosophy that directed that life. Many people (including me) believe that my father was an extraordinarily successful leader. They want to understand that success and perhaps emulate it in their own lives. For those people, The Speech is a necessary starting point.

Second, the Speech was my father's best effort to summarize his views on leadership. He sharpened, distilled, and refined it over the course of several years. As a result, it is very quotable. In fact, it is the source of many of the quotes that are attributed to my father. There is a steady stream of books about Vince Lombardi, including several books of quotes. In most of these cases, the Speech is cut up and interspersed with quotes from other sources.

But to my mind, many of those quotes don't make much sense out of context. "If we would create something, we must first be something." Even in the context of The Speech, that requires some careful reflection. What is character in action? How does that relate to mental toughness? Again, The Speech is a good starting point.

But for two reasons, at least, it is only a starting point.

CAPTURING HEARTS

The first reason, of course, was the purpose for which The Speech was intended. It wasn't an exercise in logic and wasn't intended to be. When people hired Vince Lombardi to speak, they expected—and got!—a highly *emotional* pitch, delivered with great passion. When my father spoke publicly, he grabbed for people's *hearts*, as well as their minds.

He almost always got those hearts, too. His reputation preceded him, of course: People tended to take to heart what the legendary Vince Lombardi was telling them. And although he wasn't a "polished" speaker, he knew how to play to his own strengths. He was a highly physical performer, jabbing at the air with his extraordinarily long index finger, parking his hands on his hips and cocking his head for dramatic effect, and somehow turning his stocky build, gravelly voice, and New York accent into credibility-builders.

I mentioned the fact that my mother joked about hearing The Speech thousands of times. She also said that no matter how often she heard it, it never failed to move her. Obviously, thousands of other people were equally moved.

Given The Speech's primary purpose—inspiring, motivating, capturing hearts—it's not surprising that it leaves a lot of questions unanswered. My father fudged the question as to whether a football coach had much to say to high-powered corporate leaders. (He merely claimed to have learned a few things "trampling grapes" in a "local vineyard.") He claimed that football was "like war" and "like life," but didn't go far beyond making those assertions. He made some bold imperative statements about honesty, performance, mental toughness, love, character, will, and discipline, but didn't give his audience much of a sense of how someone should *act* on the basis of those bold statements.

Like all great speakers, in other words, he left his audience asking for more. In fact, many organizations asked him to come back repeatedly. Nobody seemed to mind that The Speech didn't change much from year to year. They wanted inspiration, and Vince Lombardi gave it to them.

Inspiration is essential, like air and food. But I think there is even more to be gotten out of my father's words and deeds. I think there is a Lombardi leadership model, which managers can use to position themselves and their organizations for success.

A THINKER AT WORK

The second reason The Speech doesn't give us the complete picture is that my father wasn't the kind of person to spend weeks or months lining up his thoughts to make a bulletproof argument. That wasn't how he chose to spend his time.

He was a thoughtful person with a quick mind, trained mostly by Jesuits. He thought and worried about deep issues, including the sometimes conflicting demands that were imposed upon him by his faith and his career. (Faith called upon him to be patient and forgiving; football required him to be impatient, tough, and relentless.) He was fond of the classics and enjoyed playing Latin word games with his old parochial school buddies. He read voraciously.

As I see it, this is all evidence of an active and fertile brain. But it would be a stretch to call him an "intellectual." He was far too impatient to count angels on the head of a pin. And more important, he was paid to *lead*, rather than to think about leading. He was paid to deliver results. So it was unusual for him to sit around and come up with intellectual arguments as to why things should or shouldn't be done in a certain way. Far more often, he figured out how to move people from here to there, and then he *moved* them. And although he cast a long shadow and left big footprints, he didn't write a lot down. Unfortunately, he didn't leave us a road map.

But the lack of a road map doesn't mean that there was no system to my father's particular brand of leadership. In fact, there was a model that consistently guided his activities and made him the leader that he was. And if we look at the many clues he left us—

and are willing to read between the lines when necessary—I believe we can puzzle out the essentials of that model.

THE LOMBARDI LEADERSHIP MODEL

The model began with self-knowledge. Consider the following:

One of our goals in life has to be to know ourselves, as the ancient Greek axiom put it. It is the first step toward self-improvement.

My father had a strong sense of self. He gave a great deal of thought to issues like purpose, truth, faith, humility, and compassion. He cultivated these qualities in himself and tried to live them.

LOMBARDI RULE #1

Know yourself.
This is wisdom that is as old as mankind.
You can't improve on something you don't understand.

Sometimes—as we'll see in later chapters—he came up a little short in one or another of those qualities. In other words, he was human like the rest of us. He worried about his shortcomings and sometimes went to great lengths to mend fences with people whom he had offended. But the larger point is that he used these opportunities to learn more about himself.

If I had to do things all over again, I think I would pray for more patience maybe, and more understanding.

Self-knowledge, in turn, is the central building block for *character* and *integrity*. My father had deep reservoirs of both, more than anyone else I've ever met. As he saw it, the word "character" was a stand-in for things like belief, habit, courage, sacrifice, responsibility, hard work, discipline, mental toughness, and willpower.

LOMBARDI RULE #2

> **Build your character.**
> Character is not inherited; it is something that can be,
> and needs to be, built and disciplined.

Here's an excerpt from a letter he wrote to the players after the
1962 championship game:

> *I was extremely proud of our conduct during the
> Championship game. We never lost our poise under what
> were very trying conditions. The Giants tried to intimi-
> date us physically, but in the final analysis, we were men-
> tally tougher than they were and that same mental tough-
> ness made them crack.*
>
> *Character is the perfectly disciplined will, and you are men
> of character. Our greatest glory was not in never falling,
> but in rising when we fell.*

Clearly, leadership is more than just character. There can be no
leader without "followers." (And we are *all* followers, at one time
or another.) And people don't follow managers who don't act with
integrity.

> *The difference between men is in energy,*
> *in the strong will, in a singleness of purpose,*
> *and an invincible determination. But the great*
> *difference is in sacrifice, in self-denial, in love*
> *and loyalty, in fearlessness and in humility in the*
> *pursuit of excellence and in the perfectly*
> *disciplined will. Because this is not only the*
> *difference between men, this is the difference*
> *between great and little men.*

Also, leadership, whether in sports or business, grows in large part out of *competence*. And in football at least, competence is measured in wins and losses. A winning record gives you lots of latitude; a losing record gets you fired.

LOMBARDI RULE #3

Earn your stripes.
Leaders earn the right to lead. How?
They manifest character and integrity, and they get results.

"He can be the way he is and get results," Redskins back A. D. Whitfield once commented. "Nine hundred and ninety-eight out of a thousand would try it his way and get nothing. Lombardi is the master of his technique; the others are just beginners at it. They lack something, and when those others start carrying on the way Lombardi does, you just say, 'Ah, the hell with you, buddy.' But you don't rebel against Lombardi. His method is worth it, because you win. Players under him have never experienced a losing season. He knows what he's doing."

My father had a succinct way of putting the same thought:

No leader, however great, can long continue unless
he wins battles. The battle decides all.

Perhaps my father's most famous quote—which I'll return to in a later chapter—was "Winning isn't everything; it's the only thing." This quote conjures up a bad picture in some people's minds. They envision an out-of-control father at a Little League game, yelling at his son for not being a winner, or an overheated coach berating the kids on a Pop Warner football team.

Believe me, that wasn't what my father was about at all. The following excerpt makes his point far more effectively, I think:

There is something in great men that needs a head-to-head combat. I don't say these things because I believe in the brute nature of man, or the violent nature of man, or that man must be brutalized in order to be combative. I believe that man's greatest hour, in fact his greatest fulfillment, his finest fulfillment—is that moment when he has worked his heart out for a good cause and lies exhausted, but victorious, on the field of battle.

Victory on the field of battle is in part the outgrowth of a *comprehensive vision*. It's not enough to have character and competence; you also have to have the Big Picture constantly in mind.

LOMBARDI RULE #4

Think Big Picture.
The Big Picture is your road map and rudder. It can't change in response to minor setbacks. But it *must* change as the competitive environment changes.

You have to understand how the Big Picture must change in response to changing circumstances; but you also have to protect your ultimate goals from unnecessary alterations:

The difference [between a good coach and an average coach] is knowing what you want, and knowing what the end is supposed to look like. If a coach doesn't know what the end is supposed to look like, he won't know it when he sees it.

Leadership grows out of self-knowledge, character and integrity, competence, and a comprehensive vision. When these building blocks are in place, the leader can move individuals and organizations. In my opinion, the key to my father's success was his extraordinary ability to get people to go beyond themselves— to give more to the cause than they ever believed they were capable of giving. He did this through his personal example of enormous energy and unflagging commitment. He did this by embodying the high standards that he wanted to see in others. He did this by bestowing or withholding his approval. When you got that smile, that pat on the back, that "Attaboy!", it made all the sacrifice and the hardship seem worthwhile. And the next day, you'd start all over again, working to win his approval and avoid his disapproval.

I know this is what motivated his players, and it's certainly what motivated me. What's amazing to me is that some 30 years after his death, a lot of the players and I are still "seeking his approval." In the back of our minds, we're checking our plans and their execution against his demanding standards. Is this the way *he* would have done it or would have wanted us to do it?

LOMBARDI RULE #5

Leaders are made, not born.
Leadership grows out of self-knowledge, character and integrity, competence, and a comprehensive vision. When these building blocks are in place, the leader can lead.

Of course, The Speech and my father's various other spoken and written commentaries touch upon many more leadership-related subjects, including, for example, the relationships between teaching, coaching, selling, and leading; how winning organizations are built; how people and organizations can be inspired and motivated for success; and the prizes and pitfalls inherent in winning. In later chapters of the book, I'll lay out perspectives—my father's and my own—on these and other leadership-related topics.

First, though, we should look closely at self-knowledge, character and integrity, competence, and vision. Why? Because these are
the leadership qualities upon which everything else rests.

As an individual living in a community, aren't these the qualities
that you want in your neighbors and in the civic-minded volunteers
who sit on key town boards?

As a parent, wouldn't it fill your heart with joy to know that
your teenagers and grown-up children have these qualities?

As a manager, wouldn't your job be infinitely easier if the people working with you embodied these qualities?

As the owner of a business, wouldn't it be great if these were the
qualities that your customers thought of, when they thought of
your business?

As citizens, don't we want these qualities to motivate (and con-
strain) the people who lead our nation?

THE LOMBARDI RULES

The winning model

Know yourself.
This is wisdom that is as old as mankind.
You can't improve on something you don't understand.

Build your character.
Character is not inherited; it is something that can be,
and needs to be, built and disciplined.

Earn your stripes.
Leaders earn the right to lead. How? They manifest
character and integrity, and they get results.

Think Big Picture.
The Big Picture is your road map and rudder. It can't
change in response to minor setbacks. But it *must* change
as the competitive environment changes.

Leaders are made, not born.
Leadership grows out of self-knowledge, character and
integrity, competence, and a comprehensive vision.
When these building blocks are in place, the leader can lead.

Chapter 3

Self-knowledge: The First Step to Leadership

The value of all our daily efforts is greater and more enduring if they create in each one of us a person who grows and understands and really lives. Or one who prevails for a larger and more meaningful victory—not only now, but in time and, hopefully, in eternity.

After Vince Lombardi stepped down as head coach of the Packers, he began looking for something to do with the next phase of his life. He was in his late fifties, vigorous and apparently healthy, and still brimming over with energy. In addition, he was now a national celebrity. Not surprisingly, some Wisconsin power brokers approached him about running for either the U.S. Senate or the governorship of the state.

> *I gave it some thought. I wasn't sure my*
> *nature was right for it. You know, I'm pretty*
> *sensitive to what they say about me in the sports*
> *pages. I wasn't sure I could take the beating you*
> *get in public life. At the same time, I liked to think*
> *I could make a contribution to people. And then*
> *I was asked to go with a lot of big corporations,*
> *and that tempted me, too. You like to think*
> *you can rise to a new challenge. But I wasn't*
> *sure about those things.*

Ultimately, of course, my father decided against running for elective office, and he didn't associate himself with the business community either.

I use this quote to illustrate that my father made decisions based on his understanding of himself. He knew something about what he didn't like (getting beat up in the press), he knew something that he did like (making a contribution), and he seems to have had an understanding that the corporate arena might not have been the right place for him.

LOMBARDI RULE #1

> **Leadership begins with self-knowledge.**
> Life decisions can be good decisions only if they
> hit your own personal bedrock.

The Lombardi leadership model begins with self-knowledge, which I will define as an awareness and a wisdom about your own character and potential, acquired through experience. The opposite of self-knowledge is ignorance, misconception, and misunderstanding.

SELF-KNOWLEDGE: HOW AND WHY?

Sometimes, when I raise the subject of self-knowledge in the course of one of my speaking engagements, I see somebody in the fifth row roll his eyes, or start to fidget in his seat, or check his watch furtively. The body language sends a clear message: *I came here to hear about leadership. I wasn't expecting soft, touchy-feely stuff.*

In my opinion, self-knowledge is anything but soft; it is hard-core, bottom-line stuff. Self-knowledge is important because it is the source of informed and creative action. When we know ourselves, we know where we need to work on ourselves.

> *Every little knowledge about ourselves calls for*
> *corresponding endeavor for improvement.*

Self-knowledge is important because leaders bring their attitudes, perceptions, prejudices, and opinions to their communications, relationships, and interactions with others. We see life, people, and events *through the lens* of our thoughts about them. We see what we expect to see, hear what we expect to hear, and think the way we expect to think. We comprehend the world not as it is, but as *we are*.

LOMBARDI RULE #2

Self-knowledge comes (only) from self discovery.
A journey of a thousand miles, said the ancient Chinese proverb,
begins with one step. Take a step.

Self-knowledge is a condition—an end point (although always a moving target) and a critical prerequisite to character and integrity. How do we get there? We achieve self-knowledge through a process of self-discovery. This process involves asking questions like the following:

- What am I about?
- Where is my faith?
- Where is my spark?
- What is my life worth?

When we succeed in answering these and similar questions about ourselves, we will understand better the values and principles we believe in and also the existing strengths we have to build upon. These are the roots of maturity, effective priority setting, and good decision making. As my father put it,

> *Emotional maturity is a preface for a sense of*
> *values. The immature person exaggerates what is*
> *not important.*

The process of self-discovery and the accumulation of self-knowledge creates *an integrated identity (or personality) apart from the workplace*, and I believe that this identity is critically important. Why? Because when our identities are completely intertwined with our work lives, we lose our independence. We limit our access to our creativity. If we have no identity separate from our work identity, we don't take risks. (If I lose my job, I lose everything.) We become less passionate, and—even worse!—more cynical.

If that's not persuasive, try this: As a leader, you can't build a team, a department, or a company that is a whole lot different from who you are. The inventor can't take himself out of the invention, even if he or she wants to.

> *A team expresses a coach's personality and*
> *its own personality, and this doesn't change*
> *from week to week.*

Well, that quote begs the question, *Who are you?* What are your principles and values, and what is your purpose? "Purpose" can't be defined as what you *do*; it's who and what you *are*. So what are you? Without self-discovery and self-knowledge, you don't know.

LOMBARDI RULE #3

You can't build a team that's different from yourself.
So be honest with yourself and honest with your team.

"The successful man is himself," my father used to say. "To be successful, you've got to be honest with yourself."

People have an unerring nose for dishonesty, fraud, pretense, and posturing. You can't fake it. When faced with a crisis, a leader must draw on resources from within to meet the challenge. This is tough to do if you don't know your inner strengths. So it is vitally important that you determine your principles, who you are, what you stand for, and what your strengths and weaknesses are—in other words, self-knowledge.

That means that you have to discover and work with your own model. You can't be Vince Lombardi, nor should you try. You should be you.

> *In all my years of coaching, I have never been successful using somebody else's plays.*

In business, it is incumbent upon each of us to figure out our own "plays."

WHAT AM I ABOUT?

Perhaps you're in a work environment in which people already take self-discovery and self-knowledge seriously. If so, congratulations! A relatively newfound interest in these topics is one of the concrete benefits that grew out of the wholesale self-scrutiny undertaken by individuals and institutions in the 1980s and 1990s. This impulse was fueled by the arrival on corporate doorsteps of a new breed of worker—sometimes tagged with the label "Generation X"—who, among other things, insisted on putting first things first. If your company is already providing tools for self-discovery and self-knowledge, use them.

But let's assume, for the moment, that you're on your own. Then, for you, self-discovery will be a do-it-yourself project. You will have to conduct your own investigation, using your job and the rest of your life as grist for the self-discovery mill. If the question is, *What am I about?* then where should the answer come from?

Among the paths to self-discovery are prayer, meditation (or some other "centering" discipline), keeping a journal, dealing with hardship, and committing to continuous self-renewal. Each of these techniques has been the subject of many good and bad books; in this context, I'll just run through them and suggest how they may be useful, separately or in combination.

Prayer can take as many different forms and hold as many meanings are there are people. "An intimate friendship, a frequent conversation with the Beloved," is how St. Teresa of Ávila defined prayer. "Elevation of the mind to God" is what prayer meant to St. John of Damascus. An Islamic proverb holds that to pray and to be a Muslim are synonymous.

Obviously, this is highly personal ground. I submit to you, though, that self-discovery comes more easily when we acknowledge something that is bigger than ourselves—something that transcends our own egos.

The greatest gift my father gave me was the example of his faith. (I will have more to say about faith in Chapter 4, when we look at character and integrity.) His faith in God was his center, the source of his strength. He never wore it on his sleeve, and he never preached. A faith as strong as my father's doesn't need to be pushed on people; it was simply there, speaking for itself, making its point by its example.

He refused the entreaties of journalists to allow them to photograph him praying in church. He suspected that such a picture would lend itself to abuse by a hostile editor, and he didn't want to cheapen his faith by appearing to be trading on it.

But more to the point of this chapter, Lombardi's faith was a personal tool for discovery, challenge, and renewal.

> **When we place our dependence in God, we are unencumbered, and we have no worry. In fact, we may even be reckless, insofar as our part in the production is concerned. This confidence, this sureness of action, is both contagious and an aid to the perfect action. The rest is in the hands of God—and this is the same God, gentlemen, who has won all His battles up to now.**

In that quote, my father accentuated the positive. But I know that he also used prayer to conduct a dialogue with his Creator about the most difficult paradoxes and contradictions of his life. He was famous, and some people clearly idolized him, but he was convinced that he was unworthy of this kind of adulation. He set extraordinarily high standards for himself and those around him, but was well aware that all humans (including himself) were fallible and unlikely to measure up to those standards. He wasn't comfortable being the "tough S.O.B." side of his character—he was painfully aware of how far removed it was from "Christ-like" behavior—but he also knew that playing the Tough Guy was largely responsible for his success. Bart Starr said it best: "If you heard Coach Lombardi at practice every afternoon, you knew why he had to go to church every morning."

Self-discovery involves wrestling with these kinds of demons. Self-knowledge leads you to a state of peace that comes from your understanding of who you are and what that means.

Prayer, as noted, is only one tool for self-discovery. A *centering practice*, such as meditation and other disciplines associated with eastern philosophies and religion, is another. This is no more and no less than *paying attention* in a particular way: on purpose, with intention, in the present moment, nonjudgmentally. Some people describe it as "making your mind quiet"; more accurately, it's a technique for finding the quiet that is already there.

"All men's miseries," the French philosopher Pascal once wrote, "derive from not being able to sit quietly in a room alone." The pressures of life, the sometimes terrifying ups and downs of our family relationships, and the demands of our work pull us apart. Quiet and solitude help us put ourselves back together.

Centering practices let us sit quietly in a room alone. They help us quiet the din, and put ourselves back together. If you want to learn more, I recommend Jon Kabat-Zinn's *Wherever You Go, There You Are*, Fr. Thomas Keating's *Open Mind, Open Heart*, and Thich Nhat Hanh's *The Miracle of Mindfulness*.

Keeping a journal—a daily analysis and evaluation of your experiences—is an excellent way to reflect upon your life and discover

things about yourself. If you are not reflecting, as s<
said, you are not thinking. On a superficial level,
makes you think about how you express things and g
chance to look back on assessments you made weeks ___ months
earlier. (This is almost always revealing and sometimes humbling.)
More fundamentally, keeping a journal helps you tap into your
unconscious thought processes and make connections that you
might not make otherwise.

In short, keeping a journal helps you find out what's in your
heart. This is not always good news; again, self-discovery is a sometimes rocky path to self-knowledge.

Dealing with hardship may seem like an odd "technique" for self-
discovery: We rarely go out in search of hardship, pain, trauma, or
heartbreak. However, they often come in search of us, and when
they do, they can provide invaluable learning experiences. In the
presence of boundless, unbearable pain—the loss of a loved one,
one's health, or one's career prospects—we experience a sense of
powerlessness. But it's at such a moment, when we acknowledge
that powerlessness and recognize that there are things we simply
can't control, that we become open to profound learning. In the
face of great pain, when perhaps for the first time in our lives we
are forced to admit we don't have all the "answers," we can begin
to ask the right "questions."

Pain (of any type) is a powerful centering force. It pushes us
where good times almost never lead. As we suffer, we grow wiser.

> **Adversity is the first path to truth. Prosperity is a
> great teacher; adversity is greater.**

"To have become a deeper man," Oscar Wilde once wrote, "is
the privilege of those who have suffered." I will have more to say
about reacting to adversity in the next chapter, when I examine the
issues of character and integrity.

The last technique for self-discovery that I want to present here is *continuous renewal* (or "constant reinforcement," as I have termed it in other books I have written). This is a process that is more often associated with organizations than with individuals, but I find it a helpful concept on the personal level. "Continuous renewal" is an umbrella term for anything you can do to keep in touch with your life purpose amid the hustle and bustle of your daily life. It's a way to pick yourself up and give yourself a boost when there's no one else around to do that for you.

All of us get down, and all too often there is nobody around to pick us up. Throughout history, individual leaders have gone through personal crises that could be described as their "desert experience." At this low ebb, they become discouraged and confused. They feel that they've lost their way and that their particular struggle may not be worth the cost.

A trap we so often fall into is that, when we hear or see something that encourages or motivates us, we simply note it and go about our business. The problem is, that's not enough to keep you positive and goal oriented, as a leader must be. *The will to win— the will to achieve—goes dry and arid without continuous renewal.* Continuous renewal is a "discipline" that each person fashions for him- or herself. It might be time spent in prayer, worship, meditation, exercise, journaling, or listening to music, or it might be time spent close to nature, reading the biographies of people you admire, or consuming self-help books and tapes. What is called for is a disciplined approach to this "discipline." Every day, every week, a leader should engage in some of these things.

> **What we do on some great occasion will probably depend on what we are; and that will depend on previous years of self-discipline.**

Successful coaches like Vince Lombardi place great emphasis on practice. They run the same plays over and over, so that the players can almost run those plays in their sleep. Of course, that is exactly what the coach is striving for. What the coach wants is for the plays to be so internalized by the players, that at the crucial moment of the big game, they will react instinctually, habitually, correctly. Because if the players have to think about it too much, the game will pass them by.

LOMBARDI RULE #4

Find your own tools.
Different people get places by different paths.
Self-discovery is nothing if not personal.

It's the same for you as it is for those players. When faced with your next crisis as a leader, you aren't going to have time to do an attitude check! You are going to have to act instinctively and correctly. You bring yourself to this state through continuous renewal. Each day, you engage in some part of your discipline, so that over time you begin to internalize your purpose—the principles and values you believe in—as well as the leadership qualities and characteristics outlined in a book like this.

THE IMPORTANCE OF PURPOSE

The endgame of this search for self-knowledge is to become a person with *purpose*.

Purpose can be defined as the ideal that we keep in front of ourselves to direct our plans and actions. It is the point toward which our efforts are directed. Are we born with purpose? Do we discover our purpose? If we discover our purpose, do we choose it? In varying degrees, all three are true: Purpose is a choice, but it can also be an intuition, it can be answering an inner voice, it can be a yearning.

A vocation can be a purpose; a career cannot. "Vocation" comes from the Latin verb *vocare*, "to call." A vocation calls to you, is your calling. "Career" is derived from the French word for racetrack, which brings to mind the image of horses racing in endless circles getting nowhere. The vocation or the purpose endures; the career most likely goes through dramatic evolutions, sometimes forced upon you by outside circumstances.

Vince Lombardi was both lucky and unlucky when it came to finding his purpose in life. Coming out of college, he had no idea what he wanted to do next. He tried law school and hated that. He worked for a collection company. Then he got a call from a former college teammate, asking him to come and help coach football at St. Cecilia's High School in Englewood, New Jersey. It was a call that turned out to be a calling.

> *I'm not better nor less than the next man. But the thing about me is that I always knew what my acts would mean. I was lucky. I fell into football, really. I had some early success at coaching in high school. . . . I knew then, as a young man, the path I had to follow. Now, the earlier in life you know your track, the better off you are. I was lucky and found a singleness of purpose early on.*

What my father went through was a process of self-discovery, not only at law school and the collection agency, but also at St. Cecilia's and his subsequent places of employment. He learned something from the paths he didn't follow, and he also learned something about a path that seemed to be open to him: coaching football.

But I think he was stretching it a bit to say that he found a "singleness of purpose" early on. In fact, when he took that first job at Saints, he took it mainly as a teacher, rather than a football coach. He enrolled in courses at a nearby college to make himself a better teacher, and he tried to sharpen his skills in the classroom throughout his eight-year stint at St. Cecilia's.

> *I believe I wanted to be a teacher*
> *more than a coach.*

Throughout his life, it seemed to me, Lombardi struggled with the distinction between coaching and teaching. (See Chapter 6 for more on each of these vocations.) He often blurred the distinction between the two, and it's likely that much of his success in later life came from finding a way to integrate those two interests into a single purpose. When he strayed from that purpose—which he did when he stepped down as the Packers' head coach after the 1968 season—the self-discovery process began again.

Reflecting on why he got back into coaching a year later, he describes in poignant detail how he felt the day when it hit him that, for the first time in 30 years, he was no longer a football coach. In other words, he described the plight of somebody who has left his purpose behind:

> *It was absolutely the best off-season I'd ever had—*
> *until exactly July 15, the day they came back to*
> *start practice. . . . My God, one minute I'm going*
> *to play golf that afternoon, and the next thing I*
> *know I'm canceling the round. I find I can't stand*
> *to stay away from practice, and I'm down there,*
> *trying to stay off to the side and kind of aloof, so I*
> *wouldn't be in the way. But I couldn't force myself*
> *to do anything but go down and watch practice.*
> *And, of course, I knew right then that I had made*
> *a horrible mistake by leaving coaching.*

Why is purpose so important? I think that purpose satisfies three universal drives within each of us. It allows us:

- To connect deeply with the spirit of life that dwells within each of us,

- To express our unique gifts and talents, and
- To feel that our lives matter.

LOMBARDI RULE #5

Link goals to purpose.
A goal without a purpose is like a boat without anchor.

Most motivational speakers and authors—myself included—place special emphasis on *goals.* "Without personal and professional goals," I tell my audiences, "we wither and we die." But goals don't float in space. They must be anchored in the bedrock of conviction, meaning, and purpose, because without this foundation of purpose, we're all too likely to throw our goals overboard at the first sign of adversity.

Without purpose, we fail to connect with our core, our driving force. Without purpose, life is soft and always in danger of falling apart. Without purpose, we can't use the tools that God has given us. And without purpose, we don't have a way to make a difference. And by this, I mean a difference *through* and *to* others.

It's an interesting paradox. To find purpose, you go *within* yourself. Your life's purpose is intimate, proprietary. To realize purpose, you must go *outside* yourself. You create purpose—on purpose. Purpose becomes real—is "realized"—only when it goes public.

How do we discover purpose? In part, a sense of purpose grows out of the questions we ask ourselves. For example: "Am I going to allow my life to be governed by daily activities, or do I choose to live my life in accordance with noble principles?" True, the car needs to be inspected, the baby needs to be changed, the laundry is piling up, and the grass needs mowing. But do these day-to-day needs always have to shove higher order concerns to one side? *Always?* In other words, do I have an overriding purpose in my life, a purpose that is vivid and precise, a purpose I am committed to, a purpose that underscores everything I do? Or am I avoiding commitments in my life, by filling my life with daily activities?

In a celebrated line from their book *First Things First*, authors Stephen R. Covey, A. Roger Merrill, and Rebecca R. Merrill make the case that "the main thing is to keep the main thing the main thing." We can identify the "main thing" only by asking good questions and giving ourselves the quiet time necessary to seek the answers. For example:

- What do I do well?
- What do I so love to do that, when I'm doing it, I lose all track of time?
- What do I do that's urgent, but not important?
- Does that leave me time for the things that are important, but not urgent?
- What's the first thing I'd change about my life?
- What's the last thing I'd change about my life?

LOMBARDI RULE #6

Ask yourself tough questions.
Purpose and self-knowledge come from the answers
to tough questions—and the time to answer them.

How do you want to be remembered? What will outlast you? What will continue after you are gone?

On the day you're cremated or buried, what's going to be happening at your house? When your spouse, your kids and their spouses, your grandchildren, and your friends and business associates begin to loosen up and speak candidly about you, what will they say? What would you like them to say? That you had character, or that you were a character? That you were a person of courage and discipline? That you were a worrywart? That you had a sense of humor and were lovable, compassionate, and caring?

Imagine that you are looking around the room as these discussions are going on. These are the people who were closest to you in life. If you had any influence while you were alive, it surely ought to show up in this crowd. What attitudes, behaviors, and values can you take credit for?

What is your *legacy?* Is it what you want it to be?

THE ART OF *BENDING* PEOPLE

I noted earlier that people sniff out phoniness. Most people can tell the difference between what is real and what is not. They know when someone is trying to be something that does not ring true. Self-discovery leads to self-knowledge, and self-knowledge ought to protect us from making inauthentic moves as leaders. In other words, we ought to know where our strengths lie and play to those strengths. If it takes a spark to lead others, where is your spark?

Some people lead almost entirely through others. Jim Lee Howell, the Giants coach who rode herd on his assistants Vince Lombardi and Tom Landry, used to joke that his main job as head coach was to make sure that the footballs were inflated to the right pressure. This was exaggeration to a purpose, of course—Howell was very much in charge of that team—but he was also acknowledging that he did not have the personalities of his two assistants. Nor did he *need* to.

My father was at the other end of the spectrum. He was practically bursting with whatever you want to call it—intensity, magnetism, charisma. His eyes danced and sparkled. He gave off a sort of electricity, a force that made you want to be near him, but also gave you fair warning to *stay on your toes.*

In a very interesting interview toward the end of his life, Lombardi did some thinking out loud on the subjects of leading people and how he understood himself. It was this kind of self-knowledge that positioned him to be the leader that he was:

*I'm not an overly modest man. Sure, I'm humble,
but I've never been overly modest. What happened
[at Green Bay] isn't so hard to explain. A good
coach is a good coach, right? If you take all 26
coaches in pro football and look at their football
knowledge, you'd find there's almost no difference.
So if the knowledge isn't different, what's different?
The coach's personality. See? Now, how am I
supposed to explain my own personality? What am
I supposed to say? That I'm a great leader? A
mental powerhouse? That I've got charisma?*

*You cannot be successful in football—or in any
organization—unless you have people who bend to
your personality. They must bend or already be
molded to your personality. So my Redskin
coaches—Sam Huff, Bill Austin, Harland Svare,
and Lew Carpenter—were with me before, either
at the Packers or back when I was an assistant with
the Giants. Look, I know damned well I can't
coach all 640 players in the league. I'm only one
man. I can only be that one man, and I've got to
have men who bend to me.*

LOMBARDI RULE #7

Know your spark.
In your quest for self-knowledge, focus on how
you can authentically lead people.

Vince Lombardi's charisma was to some extent a God-given gift,
a way of presenting himself to the world that came naturally to him
and that was energizing and compelling to most people who

encountered him. It was also the result of his absolute *intensity* and *commitment*, a subject to which I'll return in Chapter 5.

But to an important extent, his charisma was also the result of years of thought about his strengths and weaknesses, and the careful implementation of strategies designed to play to his strengths and minimize his weaknesses—in other words, self-knowledge.

He knew himself well enough to know *whom* to bend and *how* to bend them.

LINKING PURPOSE AND VOCATION

I worry that some readers may feel that this chapter can be of benefit mainly to young people, or people who haven't taken on the trappings and burdens of being an adult, a parent, and a professional. Most people I know above a certain age have some version of a first and second mortgage, car loans, credit card payments, and a couple of teenagers who are anxious to go to an expensive private college. These people may hear the "The age-old saying, "*find something you love to do, then find a way to make a living doing it*," and say, "Yeah, well, go tell that to the bank!"

LOMBARDI RULE #8

> **See if you see daylight between purpose and career.**
> Then figure out if that's a good thing, a bad thing, or neutral.

I'm sympathetic, having come face to face with those challenges myself throughout my career. But I think that line of reasoning confuses purpose and career. Sometimes a purpose and a career are antithetical, and something has to give. (I don't think one could be, for example, both a priest and a bank robber for very long.) But sometimes a particular purpose *can* be squared with a particular career. It may take nothing more than re-examining your career and discovering a purpose you have overlooked in the past. It might be helpful to recall the words of Ralph Waldo Emerson: "What is my job on the planet? What is it that needs doing, that I know something about, that probably won't happen unless I take responsibility for it?"

"You know," my father once said to me, "the Lord has a funny way of putting you in the right place." I agree. And I also believe that, as the New England colonists used to put it, *the Lord helps those who help themselves*—those who make the daily effort to discover themselves, improve themselves, and prepare themselves for new and higher kinds of leadership.

THE LOMBARDI RULES

Self-knowledge

Leadership begins with self-knowledge.
Life decisions can be good decisions only if they hit
your own personal bedrock.

Self-knowledge comes (only) from self-discovery.
A journey of a thousand miles, said the ancient Chinese proverb,
begins with one step. Take a step.

You can't build a team that's different from yourself.
So be honest with yourself and honest with your team.

Find your own tools.
Different people get places by different paths.
Self-discovery is nothing if not personal.

Link goals to purpose.
A goal without a purpose is like a boat without anchor.

Ask yourself tough questions.
Purpose and self-knowledge come from the answers to
tough questions—and the time to answer them.

Know your spark.
In your quest for self-knowledge, focus on how you
can authentically lead people.

See if you see daylight between purpose and career.
Then figure out if that's a good thing, a bad thing, or neutral.

Chapter 4

Character
and Integrity

*The great hope of society is the
individual character. If you would
create something, you must be something.*

Self-discovery leads to self-knowledge. In the Lombardi leadership model, we build on self-knowledge to develop *character*. Combined with good habits and competence, this creates the foundation for leadership.

My father spoke often of character. I've already referred to his pre-seminary training, his rigorous education at the hands of Fordham's Jesuits, and his sustained immersion in what might be called the "secular religion" of West Point, where a code of duty and honor prevailed. I think this sequence of educational experiences, consistently focused on values, made him into the man he was. I also think it made him unusually aware of how one goes about building character.

This awareness is the product and the continuation of the process described in Chapter 3. In this chapter, we take that analysis one step further. How does one prepare to take one's self-knowledge and life's purpose out into the world?

I would say—and I think my father would have said—that one first *must build one's character.*

The word "character" is derived from older words that mean "engraved" and "inscribed." I like reflecting on these etymological roots, because they imply something important. Character, then, is who you are. It is written, inscribed, and engraved all over you. Everyone has a character, but not all of us are "*of*" character. Character is founded on unchanging principles. It is your underlying core. It has unspoken power, it is solid and resolute, and it doesn't blink. We know character when we see it, but we're not sure how to teach it. Character is learned from the people around us, our heroes and our role models.

> *Character is the direct result of mental attitude. You cannot copy someone else's particular qualifications, but must develop your own character qualifications according to your own personality.*

Vince Lombardi often spoke of his role models: his father, Harry (who had the letters of the words "WORK" and "PLAY" tattooed on his hands, finger by finger); his college coach, Jim Crowley, a member of the famed "Four Horsemen" of Notre Dame; the Jesuit priests who taught him at Fordham; West Point's Red Blaik; and NFL legends George Halas and Paul Brown.

> *West Point taught me discipline, regularity. I guess you'd say order.*

> *"Red" Blaik taught me the meaning of organization. And Green Bay taught me to be successful.*

Lombardi said that Red Blaik was the greatest coach he'd ever known, "Whatever success I have must be attributed to the 'Old Man.' He molded my methods and my whole approach to the game."

L O M B A R D I   R U L E   # 1

Write your character.
Find ways to write in your own concrete (before it sets up).

Heroes are important, not only because they demonstrate important qualities of character, but also because they compel us to examine how we are conducting our own lives. We hold ourselves up to the examples, images, and pictures that our heroes present to us. We try to be like them. Sometimes, as we acquire wisdom, we figure out why we want to be *different* from them.

> *I think it is also time in this country to cheer for, to stand up for, to slap on the back the doer, the achiever, a man who recognizes a problem and does something about it, the winner.*

There are other techniques for "writing your character," including seeking truth, finding and keeping faith, practicing humility, and showing respect and compassion for others. These are all described in this chapter. None is easy to adopt; all are important for leadership.

ALWAYS SEEK THE TRUTH

> *Faithfulness and truth are the most sacred excellences and endowments of the human mind.*

Truth is best described by its opposites: lying, hypocrisy, and deception. Truth is the foundation of character and, therefore, is absolutely necessary for a leader. Without truth, there can be no trust. And if they don't trust you, you can't lead them.

There are two aspects of truth that a leader needs to be concerned with: First, *what is true?* And second, *where is truth?*

For people with backgrounds like my father's and my own, there are objective moral principles that constitute what is true. Customs and social mores may change, but fundamental truths transcend time and cultures. And on a personal level, right and wrong are constant and unchanging. What is right today was right yesterday and will be right tomorrow.

Fundamental, basic truths arise out of personal reflection and experience. They illuminate and reinforce purpose. For example, I believe that:

- The ends never justify the means.
- Values are not culturally defined.
- Values without morality mean nothing, because you stand for nothing.
- Not all values are equal.
- Life is cause and effect. In other words, sooner or later, you *do* sit down to a banquet of consequences.
- There *are* moral absolutes, which *must* take precedence over social or economic expediency.
- Commitments are more important than self-interest.
- No self-interest is worth your reputation.
- It takes years to build a reputation, but only an instant to lose it.
- Truth is knowing that your character is shaped by your everyday choices:
  - Watch your beliefs; they become thoughts.
  - Watch your thoughts; they become words.
  - Watch your words; they become actions.
  - Watch your actions; they become habits.
  - Watch your habits; they become character.
  - Your character is your legacy.

A person who is grounded in truth does the right thing every time. When you are guided by the truth, you are the same person in private as you are in public. Looked at from the other end of the telescope, you know that what you do in private *matters*. Any talk of being able to "compartmentalize" your life, so that what you do in private has no bearing on your public life, is a fiction. You are no better than your principles. Oscar Wilde once said, "I forget that every little action of the common day makes or unmakes character, and that therefore what one has done in the secret chamber one has some day to cry aloud on the house-tops."

LOMBARDI RULE #2

> **Find the truth for your purpose.**
> A "true truth" is one that works in all aspects of your life.

What do you get with a person whose purpose is grounded in the truth? You get a person much like my father: no hidden meanings, no dealing in the shadows, no backstabbing.

> *I never tell a football team anything that*
> *I don't absolutely believe myself. I always*
> *tell them the truth. I can't even try to*
> *deceive them, because I know they'd know.*
> *I'd know, so they'd know.*

Leaders understand that, in any given circumstance, they may not be seeing or hearing the truth. As I noted earlier, we bring our prejudices, our preconditioning, and our own particular filters to our everyday interactions with others. The leader understands and deals with this problem. Leaders understand that the greatest obstacle to finding truth is the illusion that they already possess it. Leaders must be both analytical and skeptical. They must ask, *constantly*, "Where is the truth?"

Put yourself through this screen: Do you value the truth? Are the people around you eager to tell you the truth? If not, why not? Do you believe that truth is discovered, and error exposed, only through discussion and disagreement? Leaders can't get the truth unless there is a climate of openness, dignity, and mutual respect. Do you give your people all the information they need in order to do their work? Or do you parcel out the truth on the basis of your perception of a "need to know?"

Sometimes, in our search for the truth, we work against ourselves. Something happens that provokes or stimulates us, and we ask ourselves, "Have I seen anything like this before?" We scan our past experiences as we seek to characterize the present stimulus. Then we react, out of habit, pretty much the same way we reacted the last time we think we faced a similar experience. Oftentimes, the mechanism we developed to handle and cope with a situation, while satisfactory in the past, is inappropriate for the current circumstance. So, what happened in the past influences how we act in the present, often to our detriment.

For a leader, *real power arises in that moment between the stimulus and the habitual reaction*. By seizing that moment—by choosing to *act*, rather than react—the leader can effect real and positive change.

LOMBARDI RULE #3

Act; don't react.
Seize the initiative by seeing things for what they are.

The truth of experience is necessary for a leader. It is a wonderful teacher, but only if you reflect upon and learn from your experience. Unless you do that, your reaction is only repetitive motion. Leaders who don't learn from their experience may re-create some successes, but they are just as likely to make the same mistakes over and over again. The worst case? The leader who is locked into bad habits, resists change, seeks comfort in repetition, and applies old solutions to new problems.

While statistics are interesting, they're all in the past.

Coach Lombardi valued experience, and he studied the past to discover the truth. As he prepared to play a particular opponent, he would study films of previous games the Packers had played against that team, as well as the film of that team's game (against a third team) the previous week. This was a good and necessary invest-ment for putting the game plan together.

But Lombardi and his staff also knew that this week's opponent was *changed* from what they were the last time the Packers played them. For that matter, the Packers were also a changed team. Relying too heavily on past experience was dangerous. What had worked in the past against this opposing team might not work this week, because the other team's coaches were also studying the films, making adjustments, and seeking to create some sort of edge for their players.

LOMBARDI RULE #4

Study the past; live in the present.
Find yesterday's lessons, but assume that today is new.

So while he took care to study the past, Lombardi made sure that his team functioned in the present. In pro football, he knew full well that living in the past was a prescription for defeat. The champi-onship team that dwelled on last year's championship was unlikely to repeat that achievement. At the beginning of each post-champi-onship season, therefore, Lombardi squelched all talk about how the Packers were "defending" last year's title. *Each season*, he insist-ed, *each game*, was a new and separate challenge. Each team would have to make its own mark. Each player would have to earn his posi-tion again, no matter how well he had played the previous year.

HAVE FAITH

There are three things that are important to every man in this locker room. His God, his family, and the Green Bay Packers. In that order.

As we search for the truth, we must sooner or later confront our faith (or lack of faith) in a Supreme Being, for this is the ultimate truth. You may call it God, Spirit, the Unknowable, the Infinite, or a Higher Power.

Yes, you can choose to ignore, stifle, or suppress this aspect of your humanity, but I personally don't believe that you can deny it. I believe that each of us must come to terms with faith—knowing what we believe and why we believe it.

Spirit is an essential part of our human nature. There is something in *all* of us that yearns for the universal, the unchanging, the inclusive. We are spiritual by our nature. "We are not human beings having a spiritual experience," wrote the French truth seeker Teilhard de Chardin. "We are spiritual beings having a human experience." Many of our human problems, stresses, and illnesses arise from our persistence in ignoring the spiritual side of our humanity.

There is no situation or circumstance that is without a spiritual component. Every decision we make, every feeling we have, every relationship we nurture has a spiritual dimension. The essence of life—the growth of wisdom and love—is spiritual. And sooner or later, most of us come to this realization. To many, it happens in our forties or fifties, after we have sought joy and fulfillment in almost everything else—possessions, power, control, security, status—and found them wanting. At that point, we are finally ready to admit that true joy lies in faith, in the spiritual journey.

LOMBARDI RULE #5

Have faith.
There is no more reliable comfort and source of strength.

I've already touched upon my father's deep religious faith. Prayer and worship, as noted in Chapter 4, were important elements in his discipline of continuous renewal. He spent most of his high school years in the seminary, studying for the priesthood. He attended daily mass, and he always carried his rosary.

> ### I derived my strength from daily mass and communion.

His was not a superficial faith or a faith of convenience. It was a far-reaching commitment that touched upon all aspects of his life. On the inside of Lombardi's championship rings, for example, are two etchings. One is the Sacred Heart of Jesus; the other is the Blessed Mother holding the Infant Jesus. I can recall a number of times being in my father's hotel suite on a Sunday morning before a road game. Looking into his bedroom, I would see him on his knees, saying the rosary.

> ### We don't pray to win. We pray to play the best we can, and to keep us free from injury. And the prayer we say after the game is one of thanksgiving.

How strong is *your* faith? I don't think it's my job to convince you of anything, especially in the realm of faith. (And the definition of faith is belief *without* evidence.) But consider the following: In more than 300 studies by scientists and physicians, it has been proven that people of faith are healthier than nonbelievers. They are less likely to die prematurely. They are more likely to survive extremely stressful life experiences. Having faith evidently strengthens our immune systems and speeds our recovery from illnesses.

So am I arguing that you should become spiritual for health reasons? Of course not! That would be an untruth. You can't fake it. But if good health is the natural condition of human beings, and if spirituality leads to health, doesn't it follow that faith is also a natural part of the human condition?

From our faith comes a recognition that we possess a spirit, a soul, heart. Heart, not as in a vital organ, but an animating spirit, the source of our enthusiasm, passion, courage, zeal, energy.

It takes focus and energy to find our spirit. Spirit shapes our beliefs and values, which form our purpose. To be out of touch with our spirit, our purpose, means we aren't living to the fullest or performing at our best. Spirit gives us perspective; we come to value people over things. And from faith comes hope, not as in "optimism," which comes and goes, but hope that is steadfast and lasting, because it comes not from calculating the possibilities, but from a commitment of faith.

PRACTICE HUMILITY

> *Simplicity is a form of humility, and simplicity is a sign of true greatness. Meekness is a sign of humility, and meekness is a sign of true strength.*

Humility, as I want to use the word, is the quality of being unpretending. The humility Lombardi is talking about is giving credit where credit is due. If you did it, take the credit. If you had help, recognize those who helped you. For a leader, humility is the recognition that you get results only through the efforts of others. It is yet another way of embodying truth and reinforcing character.

There are two senses in which humility bears on leadership. The first is simply in understanding that even the most powerful of leaders is only a bit player on the larger stage of life.

> *Keep in mind that there are laws—independent of man's consent, ruling over reality, over nature, over man, too, whether he be willing to recognize them or not—to which we must bow, unless we think we can rule ourselves independently of the rest of nature. Egoism, in other words, must be defeated in self. The egoist is never happy.*

This is not to say that ego is bad. All good leaders have strong egos. The progress of the human race has been built upon the egos of great statesmen, scientists, soldiers, industrialists, and educators. Ego is belief in yourself. Ego is a pride that pushes you to accept nothing less than your personal best. The more we believe in ourselves, the higher our self-esteem, the more tension and anxiety we can endure on the road to achieving our goals. Ego, therefore, is closely tied to performance.

My father had a healthy ego, and it was a vital contributor to his success. In fact, it's hard to imagine a Vince Lombardi without an on-his-sleeve ego. Every time he assembled his team in the locker room, you saw it. Each time his team took the field, you saw it.

> *The trouble with me is that my ego just can't accept a loss. I suppose if I were more perfectly adjusted I could toss off defeat, but my name is on this ball club. Thirty-six men publicly reflect me and reflect on me, and it's a matter of my pride.*

But the same ego that helps leaders achieve greatness can also be the cause of their downfall. It's called *hubris*. Hubris is arrogance, an outsized sense of self-importance. Nothing will sink a leader faster than hubris, that unsaid feeling of "I know best." Ego must be tempered with humility. As author Ken Blanchard says, "People with humility don't think less of themselves. They think of them-selves less." Most of Shakespeare's tragedies revolve around this paradox. When ego becomes hubris, we in the audience know with certainty that the downfall is on its way.

It is the ego that wants the quick fix, the instant gratification. It is ego that causes a leader to dictate that others must walk the talk, while they themselves don't.

Humility is knowing that the only thing you, as a leader, can control is how you act, in the here and now. It is humbling to admit you can't control the past or the future. You may try to con-trol the different forces at work in your office, but there will come a time when you will have communicated to your people what it is you want done. You will have pleaded with, cajoled, inspired, and threatened them—and then you will hold your breathe and ask yourself, "Are they going to do what I want them to do or not?" And at that moment, it's out of your control.

Lombardi also tried to never lose sight of the dark side of ego—the ego that got in the way of truth and, therefore, interfered with leadership:

> *The ego destroys the humility in a person. Ego is what*
> *we think we are. The ego is the clamorous childness,*
> *the petulant childness, the spoiled childness.*

No one is immune to hubris. During a critical game in the 1967 season, the Packers were nursing a four-point lead late in the fourth quarter. They were forced to punt from deep in their own territory, and it was obvious that the opposing team was going to go all out to try to block the kick. Donny Anderson was the regular Packer punter and would ordinarily have been called upon to make the kick. But an assistant coach suggested to Lombardi that the team use its backup punter, Max McGee, because he could get the ball away faster than Anderson. This, the assistant coach reasoned, would minimize the chances of a blocked kick. Lombardi dismissed the suggestion out of hand: "No! Why would I want to do that? Go with Anderson!"

Anderson got the call, the kick was blocked, and the Packers lost the game. Caught by NFL Films, the coaches' exchange—combined with the game-losing outcome—has become something of a minor classic on ESPN, where it has been played many, many times.

LOMBARDI RULE #6

Be proud and humble.
Strike the balance. Flex your ego; run
from hubris; share the credit.

Like most coaches, Vince Lombardi tried to control all the variables that might affect the outcome of a game. In that spirit, before the beginning of the 1967 season, he had heating coils installed underneath the turf at Lambeau Field, where the Packers played their home games. His plan was to turn on the coils when the Wisconsin winter turned frigid, thereby keeping the turf pliant and giving the Packers good footing.

At the end of that 1967 season, the Packers played the NFC championship game in Wisconsin against the Dallas Cowboys. Lombardi had been warned by the weathermen that it was going to be cold, and he ordered the heating coils turned on for the first time. What he wasn't told was how cold it was going to be. The temperature plunged to 13 degrees below zero, and the struggling heating coils gave up. By the second half, the entire field was a sheet of ice. The game achieved immortality as "The Ice Bowl," and once again, my father got the opportunity to ponder the implications of hubris.

SHOW COMPASSION

We are our brother's keeper. I don't give a damn what people say. If people can't find work, whether it's their fault or not, you've got to help them and house them properly and try to get rid of the conditions that have held them back.

The process of building character begins within. But like purpose, described in the previous chapter, it eventually must find its home in the larger world of people. Things like character and integrity don't matter in a universe of one. So, eventually, you take your character out into the world, where your willingness and ability to show respect for others become critically important.

Recognizing the spark of divinity that exists in each one of us is crucial to the emergence of leadership. Searching out that spark, even in the most unlikely places, is the task of the leader. Leadership is love.

> *Everybody can like somebody's strengths and somebody's good looks. But can you like somebody's weaknesses? Can you accept him for his inabilities? That's what we have to do. That's what love is. It's not just the good things.*

One thing that gives me enormous pride was my father's complete lack of prejudice and bigotry. If you could play football, the color of your skin was immaterial. (The same was true if you *couldn't* play football, of course.)

And this may come as a surprise to those who think of my father as a rigid, moralistic reactionary. Your sexual preference didn't matter either. What mattered to him was what kind of person you were.

In my father's day, the most visible kind of prejudice was racial prejudice. It's more than a little shocking to look back to the state of race relations when my father finally got his chance to lead an organization. He came to the Packers already acutely sensitive to the insidiousness and the consequences of prejudice. Throughout his childhood and into his college days, he was frequently called a "wop." While a member of the Fordham football team, he was suspended by the college's president for fighting in the locker room. The cause of the fight? One of his football teammates suggested that Lombardi stand next to a third teammate so that everyone could "see who was darker." That was enough to get my father going. Both my father and his tormentor wound up in the infirmary. Vince Lombardi was convinced, briefly, that it was the end of his football career.

Of course, he survived the suspension and went on to pursue his teaching and coaching careers. But as head coaching jobs came and went, he became convinced that he was still suffering for being swarthy, ethnic, and Catholic. He felt that people whose names ended in vowels—like his own—were far less likely to get the highly visible and prestigious jobs in football.

*Whatever the reasons, the fact that I did not get
the [coaching] opportunities I felt I deserved
motivated me greatly.*

My father's chemistry was such that he took prejudice as a challenge, an obstacle to be overcome. Fortunately, he had the drive and talent to succeed at this challenge.

Let's return to racial prejudice. Through the end of World War II, there were almost no African Americans in professional football. To a great extent, this reflected the fact that colleges fed the pro ranks and African Americans were underrepresented at the college level. But racial prejudice was still a factor. Some teams, like the Washington Redskins, openly discriminated against African Americans.

My father trained as an assistant coach with the New York Giants, a team with good race relations. (Roosevelt Grier, though, later claimed that the Giants in his day had a strict quota of six African Americans, and imposing that kind of quota was a fairly common practice among most sports franchises.) When he moved to Green Bay, he knew he had a lot of work to do. Nate Borden, a defensive end, was the only African American player on the team. And more generally, the city of Green Bay, Wisconsin, was almost lily-white. There were adult residents of Green Bay who had never actually spoken to an African American person. Housing opportunities for African Americans were extremely limited. When my father traded for veteran defensive back Emlen Tunnell, an African American player, from the Giants, the Packers paid to house Tunnell in a hotel in downtown Green Bay.

Then my father set out to change things.

*If I ever hear nigger or dago or kike or anything
like that around here, regardless of who you are,*

*you're through with me. You can't play for me if
you have any kind of prejudice.*

That's what my father told the Packers the first time he called the team together. And as the Packers soon found out, it wasn't going to be an exercise in rhetoric. In training camp, he assigned roommates alphabetically, deliberately ignoring racial considerations. (This was the first time an NFL team had done so.) When a restaurant in North Carolina, site of a preseason game in 1959, made the Packers' four African American players enter and leave by the back door, Lombardi made the rest of the team do the same. After those same four African American players were forced to sleep in separate accommodations from the white players' lodgings, my father took them aside as the team was climbing onto the bus and told them,

*I'll never—absolutely never—put you guys in this
situation again. If it means we play no games down
here, that's the way it will be.*

Why did my father feel this so strongly? I've already referred to his sensitivity to prejudice. But at the dinner table one night, many years later, he told us another amazing story. One night, toward the end of the 1960 preseason, again in North Carolina, he was refused seating by a hostess. Naturally dark skinned, he was deeply tanned after many hours in the sun out on the practice field. The hostess mistook him for an African American man and turned him away.

The next time the Packers played a preseason game in the south, rather than abiding by the racist "Jim Crow" laws of that time and place, my father quartered the players at Fort Benning. Benning had no air conditioning, but it was an egalitarian Army base. It was this uncompromising attitude, as well as his swarthy Italian complexion, that led the African American players on the team to refer to my father as a secret "brother."

I can tell you how many players I have on the squad and I can tell you which ones aren't going to be here next year. But I can't tell you how many are black and how many are white.

Vince Lombardi was fair with everyone. He accepted and rejected people strictly on the basis of their individuality—what they were inside themselves. A sportswriter who knew him from his days as a high school coach once said, "There wasn't a bigoted bone in his body."

Lombardi was also honest enough to admit that other factors contributed to harmony on his teams. "One thing that's helped us," he once commented candidly, "is that we've been winning. When you're losing, it's easy to have discontented players—black and white."

If you're black or white, you're a part of the family. We make no issue over a man's color. I just won't tolerate anybody in this organization, coach or player, making it an issue. We respect every man's dignity, black or white. I won't stand for any movements or groups on our ball club. It comes down to a question of love . . . . You just have to love your fellow man, and it doesn't matter whether he is black or white. If anything is bothering any of our players—black and white alike—we settle whatever it is right away.

That comment came toward the end of his career at Green Bay, when he was already being celebrated as the most successful coach in the history of football. I include it here to make the point that, if anything, my father became only more determined to root out prejudice after he achieved success. And this was true in all aspects of his life, by the way. David Maraniss tells a wonderful story about how my father befriended members of the local Oneida Indian tribe. When school was in session, young Oneida boys would caddy at my father's country club. But when school let out, they were all replaced by local white kids. My father insisted on using the Indian caddies year-round. "Why," he asked his golfing buddies, "aren't they good enough to caddy for us in the summer if they're good enough in the fall and spring?"

I've devoted several pages to this aspect of my father's character, in large part because, as noted earlier, I'm proud of it. My father helped change the way things worked. In 1950, there were mainly "token blacks" in pro football. By 1970, a third of the players in the NFL were African American. Today, that number is around 60 percent. My father helped make that enormous and positive transition possible. And the impact of the transition was felt far beyond football. At the risk of stating the obvious, what happens when millions of Americans tune in every week during the football season to watch a thrilling game being played valiantly and expertly by men *of all colors?* Prejudice and ignorance go down; tolerance goes up.

But I've also cited my father's race-relations record here because I think it has profound implications for managers in all kinds of circumstances. The leadership benefits of "color blindness" are certainly a piece of it. Unlike some pro teams, the Packers never experienced significant racial tensions of any kind. In fact, a July 1968 *Sports Illustrated* article singled out the Packers as a model for the rest of the league when it came to race relations.

Equally important, though, are the *motivational* benefits. We respect everybody on this team. People get ahead on the basis of what they know and what they can do on the field. We don't permit factions, politics, or cliques to get in the way of doing business. If there's a problem resulting from perceived differences among groups, we solve that problem by getting it out in the open immediately.

Maybe to some readers, especially young ones, this all sounds like yesterday's newspaper headlines. Isn't discrimination based on race a thing of the past? My answer would be, *Yes, from a legal standpoint.* But I don't believe we've overcome four centuries of racial abuse and prejudice in four decades. Those vestigial poisons are still lurking in the corners of many organizations, just waiting for the opportunity to erupt.

Looking more broadly, are you sure that your organization doesn't discriminate against women, gays, older people, or handicapped people? As a leader, are you willing to make the kind of strong statements my father made about *loving* people who are out of the organizational mainstream? That's not easy in a culture in which we pride ourselves on being professional and "with it."

L O M B A R D I   R U L E   # 7

Search out and destroy prejudice.
Be the person who makes more people welcome and productive.

What about the other ways we group and slight each other, and show a lack of respect for each other? In many human cultures with relatively few individuals and in small organizations, for example, the newcomer is ostracized, isolated, and subjected to abuse of one kind or another. At college, it's the freshman. At training camp, it's the rookie. My father always worked to counter this negative human instinct. He insisted that the rookies be called "first-year men," so that they would feel a part of the team.

My father frequently talked to his audiences about the importance of something he called "love." He spoke of love with obvious urgency and maybe an extra measure of emphasis, as if he hoped it could stand in for a group of ideas and principles that don't really lend themselves well to description.

***Love is the respect for the dignity of an
individual—love is charity. The love I speak of is***

*not detraction. A man who belittles another—who
is not charitable to another, who is not loyal, who
speaks ill of another—is not a leader, and does not
belong in the top management echelon.*

This kind of talk confused some of his audiences. That confusion is pretty easy to understand. When we hear the word "love," we often associate it with romantic love. When we hear Jesus' prescription to "love one another," we accept that readily. But when Vince Lombardi says the same thing, we get a little uncomfortable. What's a rough, tough football coach doing talking about soft and unexpected things like "love"?

*Every year I try to think of a new word for it
[Packer spirit]. Last winter at the Super Bowl, I
called it something I have been sorry about ever
since. When those tough sportswriters asked me
what made the Packers click, I said, "Love." It
was the kind that means loyalty, teamwork,
respecting the dignity of another—heart power,
not hate power.*

I think the word he was searching for was *compassion*. It means, literally, "suffering together" and generally implies a desire on the part of the compassionate person to help in some way. The opposite of compassion is apathy, a nonfeeling, an emotional indifference. A person who lives in a state of apathy exists on the lowest rung of humanity. In fact, he or she embodies *in*humanity.

Compassionate people care for one another, in the knowledge that we are truly more alike than we are different. We come from the same Source, which is the Source of all life. We all breathe the same air, occupy the same small corner of a relatively small galaxy. We all want more or less the same things out of life: variations upon human happiness. And we're all going to meet the same fate, ultimately. As the Italians say, "After death, all men smell the same." Don't we owe each other some compassion?

If you didn't immediately say "yes" to that last question, here's a slightly more self-interested way of stating the same argument: *If I am worthwhile and lovable, then so is everyone else I come in contact with. If they are not lovable and worthwhile, then neither am I.*

LOMBARDI RULE #8

Cultivate compassion.
We owe each other empathy. Heart power
is the strength of the world.

When you're talking about romantic love, it's probably fair enough to expect love to "just happen." But compassion doesn't just happen: Like the other leadership qualities discussed in this chapter, compassion must be nurtured and developed.

"Heart power is the strength of this world," my father used to tell his audiences, "and hate power is the weakness of the world." In order to create an organization of character and integrity, you have to lead with compassion—with *heart power*—and you have to create an environment in which the people you are leading can show compassion for each other.

THE LOMBARDI RULES

Writing your character

Write your character.
Find ways to write in your own concrete (before it sets up).

Find the truth for your purpose.
A "true truth" is one that works in all aspects of your life.

Act; don't react.
Seize the initiative by seeing things for what they are.

Study the past; live in the present.
Find yesterday's lessons, but assume that today is new.

Have faith.
There is no more reliable comfort and source of strength.

Be proud and humble.
Strike the balance. Flex your ego; run from hubris; share the credit.

Search out and destroy prejudice.
Be the person who makes more people welcome and productive.

Cultivate compassion.
We owe each other empathy. Heart power is the strength of the world.

Chapter 5

Developing Winning Habits

Work and sacrifice, perseverance, competitive drive, selflessness, and respect for authority are the price that each one must pay to achieve any goal that is worthwhile.

This is a chapter about good habits. Habits are those behaviors that get us through the routines of the day and more or less prompt themselves without conscious thought on our part. It is our habits, the manifestation of our thoughts and beliefs, that distinguish us from one another. "It seems as though the second half of a man's life," Dostoevsky once wrote, "is made up of nothing but the habits he had accumulated during the first half." My father had some pretty strong feelings about what it takes to instill good habits in an organization:

> *You teach discipline by doing [something] over and over, by repetition and rote, especially in a game like football when you have very little time to decide what you are going to do. So what you do is react almost instinctively, naturally. You have done it so many times over and over and over again.*

Where do habits come from? To answer this question, we'll have to back up a few steps. Through the qualities described in previous chapters, we clarify our purpose and write our character. A fundamental building block of character is a system of *beliefs*. Belief is your conviction that something is true, and you are in the "belief" business. It is the quality of your beliefs—*This is the kind of person I am*—that determines your habits, which in turn make up your character.

Beliefs are formed by our self-talk. We constantly engage in self-talk. When someone is talking to you, you are talking to yourself three times as fast, judging and prejudging your every action. When the conversation stops, your self-talk speeds up to six times the speed of conversation.

With this self-talk, you are constantly evaluating what is going on around you in a positive or negative manner. Your focus is not on what is actually happening to you, but on what you *think* is happening to you. Over time, this self-talk accumulates into *belief*: a positive or negative opinion of yourself and your circumstances. It is this internal picture and opinion, positive or negative, that determines your thoughts, actions, habits, and, ultimately, your character.

Of course, beliefs are only as good as the self-talk from which they are derived. (*Garbage in, garbage out*, as they say in the computer world.) But good or bad, they become the basis for *action*.

LOMBARDI RULE #1

Own your habits.
Search out and identify your beliefs and
the habits that grow out of them.

Lombardi was acutely aware of this self-talk–belief–habit connection, and he was constantly trying to influence his players' self-talk. Herb Adderley, the Packers' All-Pro cornerback, recalls Lombardi talking to him after a game against the Chicago Bears. "You just played the best game I've ever seen a cornerback play," my father told him. "This game was on national television. I'm sure the people who saw the game feel the same way. Keep this in mind, that each time you go out on the field you say to yourself, 'I want these people, when they leave here, to say to themselves that they saw the best cornerback they have ever seen.'"

> *If you don't think you're a winner,*
> *you don't belong here.*

We must make a conscious effort to be aware of, and responsible for, our habits. This allows us to overcome the bad ones and reinforce the good ones. In this chapter, I'll talk about seven habits that my father thought were particularly important: courage, sacrifice, passion, commitment, hard work, discipline, and mental toughness. They helped define him as a winner, not only in football, but in other aspects of his life as well.

> *Improvements in moral character are our own*
> *responsibility. Bad habits are eliminated not by*
> *others, but by ourselves.*

COURAGE

> *The important thought is that the Packers*
> *thrived on tough competition. We welcomed it;*
> *the team had always welcomed it. The adrenaline*
> *flowed a little quicker when we were playing*
> *the tougher team.*

Courage is the habit of mind that allows us to meet danger, opposition, or hopelessly long odds with poise and resolution.

Courage is *not* the absence of fear. Contemporary culture in America—as captured in action movies and page-turning novels—gives the impression that success comes from fearlessness. Nothing could be further from the truth. If you don't occasionally experience pressure, fear, tension, or anxiety, you'd better check your pulse. As they say, you might be dead.

Courage means *experiencing* fear, labeling it for what it is, acknowledging that you're afraid, and, if it's important enough to you, pushing ahead in spite of your fear. In some cases, courage means submerging yourself in the daunting circumstance and hanging in there until you've gotten *used to it*, *mastered* it, and your fear has abated.

All leaders experience fear (no matter what word they use to describe that condition). They feel that clutch in their gut, the rush of energy, the quickening of the heart as the adrenaline starts to surge, and the flush of capillaries in the cheeks. This is *fight* or *flight*, a legacy from our prehistoric ancestors, and it's a good thing. It means that you're getting ready for what lies just ahead of you.

> *I have been wounded, but not slain; I shall lie here*
> *and bleed awhile. Then I shall rise and fight again.*
> *The title of champion may from time to time fall to*
> *others more than ourselves. But the heart, the spirit,*
> *and the soul of champions remain in Green Bay.*

LOMBARDI RULE #2

Use your courage.
When necessary, pick flight—but otherwise, be brave. Fight!

It's very common for people—even leaders—to fall into a vicious cycle of fear. They exaggerate the danger ahead, which increases their level of fear, which in turns inflates the imagined danger still further. But resolute leaders find ways out of this trap. They acknowledge that, yes; they've screwed up before, and they may well screw up again, and they may in fact screw up this time. But they plunge ahead. Why? Because their vision of what lies on the other side of the danger is big enough, vivid enough, and compelling enough to justify the effort. The desire for the reward overwhelms the human instinct to quit and compromise, to take the safe route.

In Chapter 4, I referred to the Ice Bowl: the 1967 championship game between the Packers and the Cowboys, during which my father's prized heating coils under the playing surface failed and the field turned into an ice skating rink. It wasn't just the weather and the failed technology that made that day memorable, of course. The Packers desperately needed a win against their archrival to have a shot at winning three championships in a row. From the outset, the pressure was enormous.

The game itself was a seesaw battle, complicated by the deterioration of the playing surface and the bone-numbing cold. Up in the broadcast booth, former Giant and then CBS color commentator Frank Gifford casually tossed off the line of the day: "I think I'll take another bite of my coffee." Down on the field, as the closing seconds of the fourth quarter ticked away, the Packers were down by three points, 17–14. They then played inspired football, driving the ball down the length of the field to the Cowboys one-yard line. But now only 20 seconds remained in regulation time. Bart Starr, who had already quarterbacked a masterful game, called time-out and came to the sideline to confer with Coach Lombardi.

The smart thing—the safe thing—to do at that point was to kick a field goal and try to win the game in overtime. But that wasn't good enough. Instead of playing it safe, Lombardi and Starr decided to try to win the game in the final seconds with a quarterback sneak by Starr. It would be all or nothing. The entire stadium held their breath as Starr took the ball and aimed for the goal line. The bold stroke paid off, as Starr crossed the goal line, giving the Packers a 20–17 victory.

When questioned later on the call, my father first gave a cautious answer: "We went for a touchdown instead of a field goal," he declared, "because I didn't want all those freezing people up in the stands to have to sit through a sudden death." The reporters weren't satisfied with this and pressed Lombardi. "If you can't run the ball in there in a moment of crisis like that," he said flatly, "then, mister, you don't deserve to win."

"Those decisions don't come from the mind," he concluded. "They come from the gut."

Leaders can't avoid stress, fear, pain, and pressure. The pain of realizing you're not in control, admitting you were wrong, letting go of a long, and dearly, held belief. Or the fear and stress of having to make a decision without having as much information as you would like to have.

These come with the territory of leadership. In fact, there are things affecting your business that you, as the leader, *should* be afraid of. Organizational fear (as opposed to individual fear) is good. It's a great motivator. You can't be courageous without fear. Again, I'm not talking about the personal fear that debilitates you, that stifles your creativity and clouds your intuition. I'm talking about the corporate pressure that motivates you. Without that kind of stress, you're probably doing mediocre work.

Ideally, this type of thinking becomes a habit for the organization. At the least, it becomes a habit for the leader.

My father was diagnosed with cancer on Memorial Day weekend, 1970. He died three months later. At 57 years of age and at the pinnacle of his career and his profession, he was stunned to learn that the end was now so near. And yet, he accepted his fate with courage and grace. "I'm not afraid to die; I'm not afraid to meet my God now," he told a priest who was also a lifelong friend. "But what I do regret is that there is so much damn work left to be done here on earth."

One last thought on the subject of courage: The ring that the Packers wear for winning the first "Super Bowl" (although the term wasn't yet in use) has a large diamond set in a globe of gold, signifying the championship of the world. Inscribed along one side of the ring are three words denoting qualities that Lombardi pressed into the soul of his players, for these were the traits that he always wanted the team to have as habits of the mind: "HARMONY," "COURAGE," and "VALOR."

PASSION

To be successful, a man must exert an effective influence upon his brothers and upon his associates, and the degree in which he accomplishes this depends on the personality of the man. The incandescence of which he is capable. The flame of the fire that burns inside him. The magnetism which draws the hearts of other men to him.

Passion is any emotion that moves you. It can be love, hate, enthusiasm, intensity, or zeal. Lombardi was once described by a friend as having the "zeal of a missionary." And although the Packers held a special place in his heart, his passion extended into all corners of his life. He could get excited about a great dinner at a restaurant, a sunset, a family Christmas celebration, or a game of golf.

His enthusiasm overflowed. It was a passion that could be neither corralled nor fended off. "If you said 'Good morning' to him in the right way," said Giants owner Wellington Mara, "you could bring tears to his eyes." His emotional ups and downs as an assistant coach with the Giants earned him a nickname: "Mr. Hi–Lo." A colleague once criticized him for getting worked up over what appeared to be a minor football matter. Lombardi said, in response, "If you can't get emotional about what you believe in your heart, you're in the wrong business."

Hell, I'm an emotional man. I cry. I cried when we won the Super Bowl, and I cried when I left Green Bay. Now, I'm not ashamed of crying. Football's an emotional game. You can't be a cold fish and go out and coach. If you're going to be involved in it, you gotta take your emotions with you, mister.

Lombardi laughed and cried. He communicated with every emotional tool at his disposal. "I've got all the emotions in excess," he said, "and a hair trigger controls them." *Spontaneity* was a saving grace for this hair-trigger personality. He would yell at someone and five minutes later honestly not remember whom he had yelled at or why. People understood that and forgave him the excesses of his passion. But in addition, my father never allowed his passion—and here I'm talking about his anger—to become personal.

> *There's nothing personal about any of this. Any criticism I make of anyone, I make only because he's a ballplayer not living up to his potential. Any fine I levy on anyone, I levy because he's hurting not only himself but 35 other men.*

Passion and enthusiasm are the seeds of achievement. Enthusiasm is like an ocean tide. There's a certain *inevitability* about it. Passion sweeps obstacles away. To motivate people, there must be a spark, some juice, desire, inspiration. It's tough to be a leader if you can't energize your people and tap into their emotional energy.

LOMBARDI RULE #3

Embrace your passion.
Jump into your passion with both feet—and bring others along with you.

They call it "passion" today. In my father's day, it was called "emotion." No matter what word you settle on, I doubt that you could find someone who was as emotional as my father *who could still be as effective as he was.* Vision (something we will talk about in a later chapter) is important, but along with vision there must be a hunger, a yearning to achieve the vision.

Few of us are inherently enthusiastic. Even my father had to give himself an occasional pep talk. For most of us, passion must be stoked. Every day you've got to lay on some kindling, strike a match, and fan the flames of passion and enthusiasm.

If you are not passionate and excited about your work, how can you expect to enkindle enthusiasm in your people? If you can't get excited, you have three choices:

- Do nothing and hope for a miracle.
- Get out of your leadership position so that you quit dragging people down with you.
- Engage in self-discovery and revisit your values, principles, and purpose to recapture your passion.

When I say "hate," I don't mean I wish anybody any physical harm. Do I mean I want to run out on the field and hit a man, or kick him, or fall on top of him and pummel him? No, I wouldn't do that. But I do have to build up an emotion before a game to do a good job. If I go out there feeling just fine about everything and everybody, I'm not doing the job I should.

SACRIFICE

I think you've got to pay a price for anything that's worthwhile, and success is paying the price. You've got to pay the price to win, you've got to pay the price to stay on top, and you've got to pay the price to get there.

Character takes *sacrifice*: the giving up of one thing for the sake of another. Character involves choices, and choice means sacrifice.

Despite what today's advertisements try to tell us, you can't have it all. If you decide to get to work an hour earlier to get your paperwork done before the phone starts ringing, you must either sacrifice an hour of sleep or go to bed an hour earlier (even if that means skipping the TV show you like that runs in the 10 P.M. time slot).

Throughout my father's speeches, a persistent theme is *paying the price*. This is a habit that Lombardi picked up early in life, but it was heavily reinforced during his years with Red Blaik. The intense West Point coach liked to hang inspirational signs on the walls of the Army locker room. One of them read, "Anything is ours, providing we are willing to pay the price." When Blaik published his autobiography in 1960, he titled it *You Have to Pay the Price*. Lombardi felt that great achievement required courage, determination, and drive, as well as the willingness to sacrifice when the situation demanded it.

> *A man can be as great as he wants to be.*
> *If you believe in yourself and have the courage,*
> *the determination, the dedication,*
> *the competitive drive, and if you are*
> *willing to sacrifice the little things in life*
> *and pay the price for the things that are*
> *worthwhile, it can be done.*

Sometimes my father argued for including others, such as family members, in the decision to make sacrifices in pursuit of larger goals. He was well aware of the costs imposed on a family when a person sets out to be "great." (Certainly, our family paid a price, not only in terms of the amount of time he was away, but in terms of how distracted he often was even when he was physically present.) He nevertheless was convinced that greatness was worth the cost. It stings and hurts when you fall short of a goal. The Packers didn't win every game, of course; nobody does. Sometimes you just want to crawl into a corner and lick your wounds. You don't want to see anyone from work this weekend, and you *certainly* don't want to go to that Tuesday morning film session with Coach Lombardi. That's the price you pay to get into the arena.

> *Once you agree upon the price you and your family must pay for success, it enables you to ignore the minor hurts, the opponent's pressure, and temporary failures.*

Character is not a matter of catching a break, or timing, or being in the right place at the right time, although, of course, luck plays a part in most human endeavors. People of character understand a basic law of physics—the law of cause and effect—and draw an analogy from the laws of human nature. We reap what we sow. Character comes at a price. Heavyweight champion Joe Frazier talks about the progress of a tough fight. You enter the ring with a plan, of course. But once the fight gets underway, things rarely go as planned. At that point, you are left to your instincts and reflexes—in other words, your training.

It's *sacrifice*, during all those hours of training, that equips you to hang in there against the likes of an Ali or a Foreman. "That's where your roadwork shows," Frazier says. "If you cheated on that in the dark of the morning, well, you're getting found out now, under the bright lights."

> *Every vocation calls for sacrifices of time, energy, mind, and body.*

My father often talked approvingly about the "Spartan" qualities of football. "When I speak of 'Spartanism,'" he explained, "I'm speaking not so much of leaving the weak to die, but I'm speaking of the Spartan quality of sacrifice, and the Spartan quality of self-denial."

L O M B A R D I   R U L E   # 4

> **Be prepared to sacrifice.**
> Sacrifice and self-denial lie behind every success.

Football distills and clarifies the choices that lie behind sacrifice. As my father readily admitted, it's a violent game, and it has to be played violently. It makes demands on players that aren't made in any other sport. It imposes pain and injury, as well as the *fear* of pain and injury. Playing careers are brutally short. (The average career in the NFL is only about four years, which, of course, figures in all those careers that last only a season or two.)

But these are not sufficient reasons to avoid sacrifice. When Lombardi first got to Green Bay, he found what he considered to be a lackadaisical attitude rampant among the players. After the first day of practice, he was completely discouraged. What could he do to turn this team around?

When he walked into the training room the next morning, he found it full of players getting treatment for a variety of minor ailments. He snapped. "Get this straight!" he barked. "When you're hurt, you have every right to be in here. When you're hurt, you'll get the best medical attention we can provide. We've got too much money invested in you to think otherwise."

"But this has got to stop. This is disgraceful. I have no patience with the small hurts that are bothering most of you. You're going to have to learn to live with small hurts and play with small hurts if you're going to play for me. Now I don't want to see this again!" And for the most part, he didn't.

In the award-winning movie *Chariots of Fire*, which depicts a group of young track-and-field athletes competing against one another for the opportunity to represent Great Britain in the 1924 Olympics, sacrifice—and the motivation that must lie behind it—is a major theme. One of the athletes, Harold Abrahamson, is competing for a spot on the team against a Scottish runner. In several trial heats, the Scot beats Abrahamson.

"If I can't win," Abrahamson complains to his girlfriend, "I won't run!"

"If you won't run," she says flatly, "you can't win."

This is a lesson most of us have learned, usually the hard way. But it's interesting to me that once we learn that important lesson, we don't seem anxious to have the people around us learn it, too. Rather, we seek to protect and shield them from the pain and frustration of mistakes and failure. So we might tell a friend or colleague, "Don't bite off more than you chew" or "Be happy with what you have."

What a disservice we do to these people and to ourselves! This thinking goes against the Lombardi way of leading, which encourages people, in fact, to bite off more than they can chew. Encourage yourself and others to reach for the stars. By striving to achieve a stretch target, a group will, in all likelihood, achieve more than they would have otherwise. And they will learn, or most likely relearn, a very valuable lesson: Without turmoil and commotion, there is no growth; without turmoil and commotion, there is no change; and without turmoil, commotion, anxiety, tension, frustration, and pressure, there is no improved performance. In other words, *you must pay the price.*

TOTAL COMMITMENT

I would say that the quality of each man's life is the full measure of that man's personal commitment to excellence and to victory—whether it be football, whether it be business, whether it be politics or government or what have you.

Closely related to the habit of sacrifice is the habit of *total commitment.* The difference is really a matter of shading. Sacrifice implies an awareness of what you're giving up, whereas total commitment implies a lack of awareness about anything except the task at hand. Total commitment means no loafing, idling, standing around, goofing off, or phoning in sick.

The essence of commitment is the act of making a decision. The Latin root for "decision" is *to cut away from*, as an incision during surgery. When you commit to something, you are cutting away all other possibilities, all other options. When you commit to something, you are cutting away all the rationalizations, all the excuses.

Coach Lombardi expected 100-percent effort, 100 percent of the time. No excuses, no rationalizations. He confessed that it was hard to define a 100-percent effort, beyond a simple statement: "It was all there was. There was nothing left." He said, with conviction, that he knew that kind of effort when he saw it. Upon arriving in Green Bay, he felt that perhaps half of the Packers gave 100 percent most of the time. To win a championship, he told them, they all had to give 100 percent, 100 percent of the time.

> *I'd rather have a player with 50% ability and 100% desire because the guy with 100% desire is going to play every day, so you can make a system to fit what he can do. The other guy—the guy with 100% ability and 50% desire—can screw up your whole system because one day he'll be out there waltzing around.*

LOMBARDI RULE #5

Demand total commitment.
Demand it first from yourself and then from others around you.

Intensity, singleness of purpose, total commitment: These were qualities that I believe had the most to do with the Packers' success. And no one worked harder, no one wanted to win and succeed more, than my father did.

He was a man who believed in himself and his methods, and he saw victories as an affirmation of himself and those methods. This singleness of purpose came in part from the fact that he had waited so long for the opportunity to be a head coach, to be the one in control. There were times, I'm sure, when he doubted that he would ever get the opportunity. He was 46 when he got the Green Bay job. Many lesser men would have given up by then. By the time he got the job he wanted, he had a lot of pent-up energy and determination to succeed.

Singleness of purpose—total commitment, intensity—is something all leaders can develop. Part of it lies in believing in what you're doing. My father fervently believed that what he was doing was very important. I can recall, a number of times, being in the house when he was away on a trip, and he came home early. We weren't expecting him until later, but you just *knew* he was in the house. You physically experienced his presence. That was the way it usually was when he walked into a room. His intensity was *electric*.

Total commitment can translate into preoccupation, of course, and this can have its comical moments. When my father was a high school coach in New Jersey, we lived in a neighborhood of post–World War II tract homes, where every house looked virtually the same. On more than a few occasions, my father came home engrossed in some problem relating to his high school team. He drove into the driveway, parked the car, and walked distractedly into the kitchen—only to discover that he was in the wrong house!

One time in New York, my mother drove my father to the train. A neighbor hitched a ride to the train with them. My father sat there, for the entire ride, lost in thought. When they got to the station, my father leaned over, said, "Thanks, honey," kissed the neighbor on the cheek, and walked over to the platform!

My mother once said that the biggest mistake she ever made was getting married during the football season. Why? Because my father rarely remembered their anniversary. One time in particular, he forgot it and caught all kinds of grief from my mother. For the next few days, he took it out on the players. The Packers all wrote down his anniversary date, so they could be sure to remind him the next time it came around.

> ### *The only way I know how to coach*
> ### *this game is all the way.*

"Everything with him is just pushing, pushing, pushing toward a goal," the Redskins' Gerry Allen once said. "He never stops, and he's gonna have it. He's gonna have it. He's gonna get it there. I don't know who's gonna be around to share it with him, but he's gonna get it, because he never lets up."

As Allen implied, leaders make commitment a clear priority, with no room for misunderstanding. Leaders find a way to weed out the uncommitted. When Lombardi arrived in Green Bay, he found very few Pro Bowl players to work with. There was one such player, a wide receiver with considerable talent. But when my father talked to that player, he got strong signals that the player's dedication and commitment were limited and wouldn't be affected by anything the coach could do. Before he ever stepped on the field, Lombardi traded the player to another team. The message to the rest of the team was clear: *If you're going to play for Vince Lombardi, you're going to do so at a high level of commitment.*

> ### *A guy may have the potential to be the best player*
> ### *of all time. He's able, agile, and intelligent.*
> ### *Yet unless he is totally committed to the team and*
> ### *victory as a unit, he won't win ball games.*
> ### *And winning is the name of the game.*

Sometimes my father's level of commitment took people's breath away. One such episode occurred when the Packers were preparing for a championship game that was going to be played the day after Christmas. An assistant coach asked Lombardi for a few hours off to do some shopping. The answer came back: "Do you want to be Santa Claus, or do you want to be a football coach? You can't be both."

Weed out the uncommitted.
The organization that wins is populated by winners.

You make a decision. You "cut away" all the other options and possibilities when you decide to be an assistant coach at the professional level. To some readers, I'm sure, banning Santa Claus sounds harsh. But it was consistent with the model being set by Lombardi himself—*he* wasn't going shopping—and it was consistent with his entire approach to coaching.

If you quit now, during these workouts, you'll quit in the middle of the season in a game. Once you learn to quit, it becomes a habit. We don't want anyone here who will quit. We want 100 percent out of each individual, and if you don't want to give it, get out. Just get up and get out right now.

These strong words usually were delivered early in training camp and almost always had the desired effects: *Weed out the uncommitted, and get the last 10 percent out of everybody else.* This certainly applies to the corporate world as well. For example, GE's celebrated CEO, Jack Welch, once said that he felt he had moved too slowly in this area, meaning that he had not moved quickly enough to rid GE of non-performers. While he could be forgiving of managers who might have missed their numbers, he was less forgiving of managers who did not live up to GE's values of passion for excellence, openness, and other Welch-like qualities that demonstrate unwavering commitment to the organization.

HARD WORK

There is no substitute for work.

My father, like his father before him, was always a hard worker. When he took the job as an assistant at West Point under Red Blaik, though, he got a new perspective on what constituted "hard work." Blaik lived and breathed football during most of his waking hours, seven days a week, 52 weeks a year. It wasn't unusual for him to reassemble his coaching staff after dinner, long after the cadets had gone off to their studies and to bed, and to watch films and discuss strategies until midnight. Then they'd be at it again first thing in the morning.

Lombardi carried these habits forward with him into his professional football career. "When the other coaches—the rest of us—would leave the Giant offices," head coach Jim Lee Howell once recalled, "there was always one light still burning, the one in Vince Lombardi's office."

Lombardi's week during the season, and that of his assistants, looked like this: Sunday was game day. Monday, the coaching staff would watch Sunday's game films from 9 A.M. until midnight. On Tuesday, they would work from 9 A.M. until 11 P.M., putting together the game plan for the upcoming Sunday. Wednesday consisted of practice and more planning from 9 to 5, then a break while Lombardi taped his T.V. show, and then two more hours after dinner. Thursday was a little lighter: practice and meetings with the assistants, wrapping up around 4 P.M. After practice on Friday, the assistants usually took off to scout a college game; they would rejoin the team late Saturday night. Sunday, it started all over again.

It means you get home a little later, a little wearier, a little hungrier, and with a few more aches and pains.

In other words, a 60+ hour week, every week between July and December (or January if the team was in the playoffs), seven days a week, with no days off, and very few excuses accepted. Lombardi sustained this grueling schedule in part because there really was that much work to be done. He was not one to make up busywork just for the show of it. (The fact that he was also general manager, as well as coach, made his own workload particularly heavy.) But he was also making a point for the benefit of his players. They all saw him put in more effort than they did, every day of every week. So they were moved to put in a little extra effort on Sundays, just to balance things out a bit.

> *The harder you work, the harder it is to surrender.*

Perhaps this statement seems self-evident to most people. Isn't it obvious that you have to work hard to get what you want out of life and to motivate the people around you?

I wish it were obvious, but I don't think it is. All too often, our culture celebrates success without effort. Our media tend to focus on people who achieve their goals in a seemingly effortless way—the "overnight successes." And our prisons are full of people who decided that they could take a shortcut to their goals and got caught.

> *If you really want something, you can have it if you're willing to pay the price. And the price means you have to work better and harder than the next guy.*

LOMBARDI RULE #7

Work at it.
Don't buy the myth of the overnight success.
Invest in your talent.

I don't believe in overnight successes. "No one who shuns the blows and the dust of battle wins a crown," as St. Basil put it. I think that most—maybe even *all*—of those people we celebrate for their effortless achievements have actually put a whole lot of time and sweat into preparing for their moment of victory. Yes, they *make* it look easy. (That's one of the by-products of preparation.) They may even *talk* in a way that makes their success seem almost inevitable. But if you listen carefully to them, you'll usually find that they are describing their pursuit of a compelling goal. It's the clarity of that goal—vivid, precise, energizing—that makes their success seem predestined.

What they're not necessarily talking about in the flush of victory up there on the stage or in the postgame interview are the long, lonely hours of practice they subjected themselves to or the many, many doubts they experienced along the way.

DISCIPLINE

I've never known a successful man who deep down In his heart did not appreciate the discipline it takes to win. There is something in great men that needs discipline, that really yearns for and needs head-to-head combat.

Hard work isn't simply the number of hours invested or the number of blisters or bruises incurred. Hard work is also *discipline*: the kind of focused training that develops self-control.

Discipline helps you make the hard decisions. It helps you embrace and endure the pain associated with change. It helps you stay on track despite stress, pressure, and fear.

Study the great performers in any field—music, theater, sport, or whatever—and you'll find that they all possess an enormous degree of discipline, a sense of duty. They have learned self-control, and they exercise it.

Fortunately, discipline is not limited to the tiny number of people who work at the peak of their artistic pursuits. Leaders are "performers," too, are they not? Not in the sense that a leader is "acting." (If you are, your people will know it, and you will lose them.) But leaders do operate "out front," on a stage, so to speak. Their "stage" is their organization, and their audience is the people inside and outside of the organization who look to them for guidance. And like other performers in other arenas, they achieve and maintain discipline through *practice*—doing the component parts of their work over and over and over until they get them right.

> *A good leader must be harder on himself than anyone else. He must first discipline himself before he can discipline others. A man should not ask others to do things he would not have asked himself to do at one time or another in his life.*

As stated earlier, Lombardi placed great emphasis on practice. He and his assistants would run the same play over and over again, literally dozens of times, with Lombardi barking out, "Run it again!" each time there was even the smallest mistake. After a while, it was the *players* who would yell "Run it again!" They were learning to *look* for mistakes, which is the all-important step that precedes *eliminating* mistakes. With practice and discipline, they were gaining complete confidence in their ability to execute this particular play.

It is this discipline of training, investing those countless hours of practice, that leads to mastery, which takes a skill from the conscious level to the subconscious level. Then you are free to let your instincts and intuition guide you. This is another leadership paradox: In leading a team or organization, discipline leads to freedom.

Too many of us equate success with freedom: the freedom to "do our own thing." Faced with an ethical challenge, we all too often respond, "Whatever." This isn't freedom; it's license. We forget that the shadow twin of freedom and tolerance is weakness and apathy. True freedom comes from having a core set of values and possessing the discipline, courage, and sense of duty and obedience to those values, so that when we are challenged, we respond almost unconsciously in ways that are in accordance with our values.

Discipline is most evident on the field, where the efforts of 11 talented men have to be perfectly coordinated. But discipline is equally important *off* the field. In *Second Effort*, the sales-motivation film in which my father played himself, he advised the insecure young salesman who was getting an informal tutorial from him to "operate on Lombardi time!" Like most of the precepts in the film, this was drawn directly from Lombardi's coaching philosophy. If a meeting was scheduled to start at 9 A.M., the Packers learned the wisdom of being in their seats at 8:50. If they arrived at 8:55, they were, in the coach's view, five minutes late!

LOMBARDI RULE #8

Be disciplined on and off the field.
Discipline takes different forms—but it always pertains.

Willie Wood, the All-Pro Hall of Fame safety, walked into a meeting one day five minutes before the scheduled starting time. But because everyone else had been *ten* minutes early, Lombardi had already started the meeting. He gave Wood a terrible chewing-out. At the end of the outburst, Wood said sweetly, "But Coach, I still have five minutes." Everyone laughed, but the point was made. Lombardi made the point in a number of ways, once cutting a player who fell asleep during a meeting. By way of explanation, my father simply commented, "Any man who can't stay awake in a meeting—he doesn't belong on the Packers."

I believe a man should be on time—not a minute late, not 10 seconds late—but on time for things. I believe that a man who's late for meetings or for the bus won't run his pass routes right. He'll be sloppy.

The discipline you exhibit in how you manage time reflects the kind of leader you are. If you constantly start meetings late or if you continually miss deadlines, you send a clear and negative message to the people around you. You send a message that you don't value and respect them, because you don't value *their* time. If you did, you would be on time.

Perhaps coach Lombardi's greatest show of discipline happened the year he retired from coaching the Packers and served solely as the team's general manager. Once the season began, he realized how much he missed coaching. The hardest thing for him to do was to observe from afar and not get involved, particularly after the team started playing poorly. With great personal discipline, he stayed away, knowing that to get involved would be unfair to the man he had hired to replace him.

My father often told his players, "Fatigue makes cowards of us all. When you're tired, you rationalize. You make excuses in your mind. You say, 'I'm too tired. I'm bushed. I can't do this. I'll loaf.' Then you're a coward." Certainly, he was emphasizing the importance of good physical conditioning. But he was making a larger point, too, that in the face of pressure and tension, unless you have developed the habit of discipline, you will quit. Stress and tension, when not moderated by discipline and a strong sense of duty, cause us to compromise and take shortcuts. Instead of doing things the *right* way, you choose to do it *your* way.

MENTAL TOUGHNESS

The most important element in the character makeup of a man who is successful is that of mental toughness.

Once, Art Rooney, the late owner of the Pittsburgh Steelers, told my father that he knew a 10-year-old boy who was about to try out for a prep school football team. Rooney asked Lombardi if he would give the boy some advice.

"Dear Tim," my father wrote in a note. "If you want to make St. Bede's football team, you must be mentally tough. Best, Vince Lombardi."

Mental toughness was one of my father's favorite topics. He believed it was the single most important skill leaders could develop in themselves and in the people around them. Mental toughness is the ability to hold onto your goals in the face of the pressure and stress of current reality. It's the ability to hold on, and hold on, and *hold onto what you want in the face of what you've got.* Mental toughness is the glue that holds a team together when the heat is on and helps that team persevere just a little bit longer, which in many cases is just long enough to outlast the opposition.

> *Mental toughness is Spartanism with its qualities of sacrifice and self-denial, also the qualities of dedication and fearlessness and love.*

I think my father's own brand of mental toughness dates back to his days at Fordham. He was an average player, compared to some of the more talented players around him. (He was probably the least celebrated of the "Seven Blocks of Granite" that made up the 1936 Fordham line.) He played, nonetheless, mainly because of his pure determination. He once played an entire game with a cut inside his mouth that required 30 stitches to close after the game. And in playing for Fordham, which depended on its tenacious defense to make up for its low-scoring offense, he learned another version of the same lesson. "I can't put my finger on just what I learned playing . . . in those scoreless games," he later said, "but it was something. A certain toughness."

As a coach, Lombardi schooled his players in the mental approach to football, telling them, "Hurt is in the mind." He stressed that in order to win, they would have to disregard the small hurts, ignore the pain, and scorn the pressure that would be applied by both opponents and backers alike. Gale Gillingham, a high Packer draft choice, was released from the college all-star game with a broken hand. Reporting to the Packers, he practiced the next day.

That toughness learned at Fordham was challenged, and I'd say reinforced, in subsequent years by Lombardi's professional frustrations. He waited a long time for the opportunity to lead a college team (and that opportunity never came). Next, as I noted earlier, he waited for a top slot in the pros. It was a long and painful drought, which my father simply had to endure.

> *Mental toughness is many things, and rather difficult to explain. Its qualities are sacrifice and self-denial. Also, most importantly, it is combined with the perfectly disciplined will, which refuses to give in. It's a state of mind—you could call it "character in action."*

Refusing to give in. Character in action. In these phrases, my father was struggling to get at something at the core of his training and beliefs. He was talking about the necessity to stay the course when things were going wrong. He was talking about using stress, or even failure, as a way to come back even stronger. We learn to persevere by persevering. "Sometimes it's good to have an obstacle to overcome, whether in football or anything," he once said. "When things go bad, we usually rise to the occasion."

Mental toughness is the ability to be at your best at all times, regardless of the circumstances. It's easy to do well when there's no pressure or stress, but how many of us can be poised when the heat is on? Mental toughness is constancy of purpose; it is total focus and emotional control. Mental toughness is not rigidity in the face of adversity; it's stability and poise in the face of challenge. Mental toughness is seeking out the corporate pressure that can't be avoided anyway and being *energized* by it. It's not the ability to survive a mistake or failure; it's the ability to come back even stronger from failure.

Mental toughness is not inherent. It's not something that people are born with. Instead, it's learned. We start small, achieving a minor goal. Then we set our sights higher and succeed again. We may not succeed each time, but if we work patiently toward our larger goals, savoring victories and shrugging off small setbacks, we will prevail. And each time we raise the ante, we gain skills and confidence that make the next success more likely. I commented earlier that habits build character. This particular cycle—hard work, success, more hard work, more success, with the occasional setback thrown in—is the crucible of character.

> *What is defeat? Nothing but education, nothing*
> *but the first step to getting better. It is defeat that*
> *turns the bones to flint and gristle to muscle and*
> *makes men invincible and forms those basic*
> *natures that are now in ascendancy in the world.*
> *Do not be afraid of defeat.*

Mental toughness is the willingness, day in and day out, to keep the commitments you make to yourself. It is "singleness of purpose," also one of Lombardi's favorite phrases. It is the ability to stay motivated, no matter what obstacles rear up in front of you.

LOMBARDI RULE #9

Be mentally tough.
Use your toughness to beat setbacks.
Use your toughness to seek out new challenges.

Mental toughness is also the determination to look forward and seek out the next challenge, pushing the organization in new directions and *acting*, rather than simply reacting. We don't persevere just to keep breathing; we persevere to prevail and, ultimately, to *win*.

And this is character in action.

THE LOMBARDI RULES

Winning habits

Own your habits.
Search out and identify your beliefs and the habits
that grow out of them.

Use your courage.
When necessary, pick flight—but otherwise, be brave. Fight!

Embrace your passion.
Jump into your passion with both feet—and bring
others along with you.

Be prepared to sacrifice.
Sacrifice and self-denial lie behind every success.

Demand total commitment.
Demand it first from yourself and then from others around you.

Weed out the uncommitted.
The organization that wins is populated by winners.

Work at it.
Don't buy the myth of the overnight success. Invest in your talent.

Be disciplined on and off the field.
Discipline takes different forms, but it always pertains.

Be mentally tough.
Use your toughness to beat setbacks.
Use your toughness to seek out new challenges.

PART II

INSPIRING OTHERS TO GREATNESS:

How to Lead Like Vince Lombardi

Chapter 6

Teaching, Coaching, and Leading

Most people in business possess a leadership ability. Unfortunately, leadership does not rest solely upon ability and capacity. That is not enough. A man must be willing to use it.

So far, the lessons of this book have focused mainly on how a person prepares for a position of leadership.

This structure was purposeful. I believe it accurately reflects what Vince Lombardi thought about leadership. Leadership, as he said many times and in many different ways, is a *process* that begins inside the individual. The individual must take responsibility for developing knowledge about him- or herself and must find a purpose through that process of self-discovery. Then he or she must build *character* on the basis of that knowledge.

Eventually, of course, the leader must go beyond him- or herself. (There is no leader without followers.) That's what the next two chapters are about. Once you have adopted the Lombardi leadership model, what comes next?

What comes next is some version of "teaching," or "coaching," or "leading." My father had a strong sense of what these words mean, and those concepts are at the heart of this chapter.

In this chapter, rather than focusing on *habits* (nouns), we will focus on *actions* (verbs). We will focus on actions like leading, building, instilling, insisting, creating, and showing. We will focus on striking the balance between closeness and distance, between being "one of the boys" and being a leader.

As we make the transition from individual responsibility to responsibility to the group, we should revisit the topic of what we mean by "leadership." For some, leadership means going ahead and showing the way. For others, it means guiding a person and bringing him or her along. For still others, it means providing direction.

So defining leadership can be a squishy business and hard to get one's arms around. You squeeze one end, and it starts squirting out the other side. One reason for this squishiness is that different circumstances call for different types of leadership. Leadership is *not* situational—I hope I've made my opinion on that clear. But to find a leader, first you must define the circumstances. For instance, military, Napoleon; intellectual, Socrates; charismatic, King David; reform, Eleanor Roosevelt; business, Jack Welch; spiritual, Pope John XXIII; and so on.

Different styles? Yes. And the strategies and tactics employed by a leader may change with the situation. But the underlying leadership qualities remain the same—that is, those qualities which bring people around the leader to a higher level of performance.

> *There are patterns of behavior that we can recognize in our employees that may help us, but each individual or group of individuals has facets that must be treated on an individual or group basis with the usual stereotype rules thrown out.*

As a leader, what is your situation today? Most likely, it involves some combination of the following:

- **Globalization.** Competition is coming from everywhere and everyone, including people and places you wouldn't have conceived of even a short time ago.
- **Technology.** Everyone has access to the same information you do; at the same time, the world is shrinking and fragmenting.
- **A new social contract.** An increasingly diverse workforce is a welcome opportunity for some and a threat to others.

In other words, there is some degree of chaos, especially compared with the orderly ways of the past. In many cases, the response to this chaos has been some version or combination of downsizing, "rightsizing," re-organizing, re-engineering, merging, or acquiring. If your company hasn't downsized, you know someone whose company has. Increasingly, organizations see people as replaceable parts, fungible. There is little loyalty from employer to employee or from employee to employer. All this tends to make people fearful, confused, cynical, or distrustful.

Far too many employees are demoralized. They actively dislike their company, citing poor leadership at the top. These employees say that their leadership doesn't understand what motivates them and complain that their efforts go unrecognized and unrewarded.

So change and challenge are the fundamentals of your situation as a leader. Change is the constant, the given. Change is everywhere, inevitable, and accelerating.

The issue for you as a leader is whether you will observe this change, react, and subsequently fail, or whether you will anticipate change and adapt to it. Will you adjust to new circumstances? Far too often, we become aware of the present only as it becomes the past. Leadership involves getting people to *adapt* to change. Leadership is motivating people to adapt in a positive, constructive, creative fashion. Leadership is creating an environment and an atmosphere within which people willingly adapt.

LEAD WITH INTEGRITY

In dealing with people, the first thing we must have is all the facts, and then we must be constructive. If we are constructive, we will be reflecting our own sincerity and dedication, as well as our personal and company integrity. If the facts indicate we made a poor decision or took an

improper action, then we must admit that we were
wrong. On the other hand, if the evidence, based
on those facts, shows we were correct, we must
stand firmly and fairly to what we believe is right.

It won't surprise the reader who has gotten this far to read again that *integrity* is a key part of the Lombardi leadership model. "Integrity" means having an upright, honest, and complete character.

In a different, but related, sense, the word means that throughout its whole, an object is of uniform consistency and strength. No matter where one applies pressure or stress, one gets an equal and consistent response. This is structural integrity.

Integrity permeates behaviors. My father referred to integrity as "character in action." You develop integrity after you have determined your principles and values. This suggests that it is an outer expression of your inner character. It is the manifestation of an unshakable set of principles that you will not violate under any circumstances.

Leaders have to impress upon those around them an idea of who and what they are. "You've got to get across to the players that feeling of truth, that feeling of honesty, that feeling of selflessness," my father once said. This means that you *do what is right*. You do what you say. You act in conformity with the values that you espouse. Your behavior is predictable, because you are consistent in your choices and your actions. As a leader, you can't be one person in private and someone else in public. Sooner or later, you are going to forget which person you are supposed to be, at a particular moment, public or private, and you will confuse and disillusion those around you.

Maybe being predictable sounds easy, at least to those who haven't yet held a leadership position. Just "be yourself," right? Well, it's almost never that easy, even when you know who "yourself" is. (See Chapter 3.) Leaders are human; they sometimes have moods that they permit themselves to indulge. And like the rest of us, they want to be liked. Conversely, they may feel the need to prove how tough they are, even when that's not what's called for by the situation at hand.

Integrity takes Lombardi's mental toughness, and it has a cost. You must weigh the depth of your commitment before you undertake to lead with integrity. You will be tested, by cynics, by those interested in the lure of short-term gains, and by those interested more in style than in substance. As a result, you'll need to make sure that you have deep enough reserves in order to act consistently as a person of integrity. (Chapters 3 through 5 were all about building these kinds of reserves.) People will be watching what you *do*, rather than listening to what you *say*.

LOMBARDI RULE #1

Be authentic.
Act your integrity. Be predictable.
Make amends when you foul up.

"Authenticity" is another word that might be substituted for integrity. My father underscored his authenticity by identifying his own mistakes, putting a spotlight on them, and asking to be forgiven. This was a good thing, too, because, being as volatile and emotional as he was, he jumped the gun on a regular basis. He would fine a player and then have to rescind the fine. He would blurt something out and then have to apologize for it.

Instead of coming across as indecisive or insincere, Lombardi came across to his players as authentic and, ultimately, fair. One day, Lombardi threw veteran safety Emlen Tunnell off the practice field for what he perceived to be a lack of effort. Tunnell was then in his late thirties, nearing the end of a celebrated career. (He was soon to be elected to the Hall of Fame.) The next morning, in front of the entire team, Lombardi apologized. What he had done, Lombardi said, was wrong, and he was sorry for it.

"It took a big man to come to me like that," Tunnell said afterward. "A helluva big man. He didn't have to do that."

Leadership ultimately rests on moral authority, and you can't have moral authority without integrity. Leadership is demonstrated on a day-to-day basis. Everything you do will be known by your followers. Therefore, you must act at the center of ethical conduct, not at the margins. Your sense of honor must be greater than your moods. Without integrity, there can be no trust—and again, if they don't trust you, you can't lead them.

BUILD TRUST

I think to be successful, you've got to be honest with yourself. You've got to believe you're just like everyone else. You must identify yourself with your associates, you must back up your associates, even at risk, sometimes, of displeasing your superiors.

Trust is what other people invest in you, based on your integrity. Trust is their absolute confidence that you are truthful and reliable.

As my father commented many times, the acid test of a leader is the existence of willing followers. How do you create willing followers? By acting with integrity, especially in a pressure situation, when such actions entail some risk to you.

Trust is earned through patient investment and long association. It can be destroyed in an instant. Leaders destroy trust in all sorts of ways, including not doing what they said they would do and not saying what's really on their minds. They do it by asking for input when it's obvious they've already made up their minds in a particular direction, or by making up an answer rather than admitting that they don't know.

Leaders destroy trust by killing the messenger. People watch their leader extra carefully when bad news arrives. The implicit question, in this a situation, is, *Is this an authentic organization?* Real organizations and real leaders can tolerate—even welcome— bad news. Inauthentic organizations and untrustworthy leaders shoot the messenger.

A leader may destroy trust by constantly asking people to do more than is possible. You can't ask people to eat nails or jump in front of trains. More often than not, though, as explained in previous chapters, the organization has room to improve. Asking for effort and improvement in ways that are honest, fair, candid, and open may actually *build* trust. If the call to extraordinary effort is perceived to be authentic, people very often will eat nails and stop trains. To Vince Lombardi, leadership was all about winning people's hearts:

> *How does one achieve success in battle?*
> *I believe it is essential to understand that battles*
> *are won primarily in the hearts of men. Men*
> *respond to leadership in a most remarkable way.*
> *Once you have won their hearts,*
> *they will follow you anywhere.*

Trust can't be decreed, demanded, or bought. It can be earned through a judicious use of authority, combined with results. When my father first arrived in Green Bay, the most common emotion he evoked was fear. This was because he seemed to be brusque, imperious, unpredictable. He seemed to be saying, arbitrarily, "There's only one way to do things—my way." Soon, though, it became clear that he had the vision, energy, and integrity to build a winning organization. It became clear that he would not abuse his authority—that in fact, he would use that authority to turn the organization around.

> ### Earn trust through investment.
> Use your authority to build the organization's trust in you.

Trust can be earned when the leader goes first. "I don't recall him ever asking us to do anything he wouldn't do himself," recalled Willie Davis. "That means a lot."

As a leader, you will be watched closely, and your every action will carry meaning for your people. Everything you do will send a strong signal, either that you mean what you say or that you don't. Actions that contradict your message will destroy trust and will be used as an excuse for not taking you seriously. Not only must you talk the talk and walk the walk, you must understand that *your walk talks.* Everything you do and everything you don't do say something about what you value as a leader. When discussing integrity and trust, I always cite the advice of Marcus Aurelius: "If it is not right, do not do it. If it is not true, do not say it."

Do you want to earn your peoples' trust? Don't ever ask anyone to do anything you haven't done before and aren't ready to do right now, ethically or organizationally.

You are the model. That means that when people come to work in the morning, your car should already be in the lot. And when they leave at night, your car should still be right where you parked it that morning. (I'm speaking figuratively, but also to some extent literally.) Understand this as a leader: Your people never take their eyes off of you. They are watching you 24 hours a day, 7 days a week, and you have to walk the talk 24 hours a day, 7 days a week.

Trust can be earned when the leader acknowledges that there is pain ahead. Almost all adaptation and change involves short-term pain and disruption. The trustworthy leader tells people what to expect, with a bare minimum of sugarcoating. In fact, people expect leaders to make tough decisions and tell them what's coming. They lose faith in those leaders if tough decisions are avoided and bad news doesn't get shared.

> *There are occasions when being hard and being tough immediately is the easiest way and the kindest way, really, in the long run. We have to be hard sometimes to get the most out of people. We have to be hard sometimes to get the most out of ourselves, and what can appear to be cruel at a particular moment can eventually turn out to be a blessing in the long run.*

As a leader with integrity, what is your biggest challenge in getting your people to adapt to change? I believe it is overcoming the fear of, and resistance to, change. Fear and resistance prevent adaptation. The barriers to adaptation are threefold:

- The individual's fear of change.
- The leader's attitude toward change.
- The organizational culture.

For most of us as individuals, change is perceived as dangerous, a threat to be avoided. We seek to maintain the status quo at all costs, mostly because it's known and it's comfortable. We invalidate any call for change by labeling it "nonsense." On the basis of little or no evidence, we say things like "Our customers aren't asking for this." We often present the appearance of adaptation, paying it lip service, without actually making any change. We discredit the messenger. We appeal to the memory of past successes. By denying the need to adapt, we experience the negative aspects of failing to change and, thus, make change even more difficult. We begin to feel victimized; we begin to place blame.

But it's not only the individual who stands in the way of change. Many leaders today are complacent, resting on past accomplishments.

Their standards are based on past success, rather than current competition. With too little external and internal feedback and a lack of candor and honesty, both with themselves and between themselves and their reports, leaders are isolated and insulated. Comfortable in their routine, they are able to render almost invisible the need to adapt. In so many words, they are saying, "We're important, people have to buy from us, so why change?"

Organizational culture, too, demands scrutiny when adaptation becomes necessary. Adaptation is triggered from the top, by the leader, but it is *achieved* only from the bottom up. The problem is that an organization will not adapt until its culture is ready. Culture is the bedrock upon which everything in an organization is done. It's what people do when no one is telling them what to do. It's the context that produces all outcomes.

Culture is the fixed, unwritten rules that set expectations, dictate behavior, and influence results. Most adaptation initiatives flounder because the culture resists anything that threatens the status quo. As a leader, therefore, you need to appreciate the extent to which your culture controls how, what, and when things get done in your company.

This next assertion may surprise you: *You can't change your company's culture.* That culture preceded you and will probably outlast you. It has a life of its own, as it is passed from generation to generation of workers. What you as a leader *can* control—and therefore change—is your company's *climate.*

Climate is that collection of policies, procedures, and incentives that govern the day-to-day operation of your company. More importantly, it is what you as a leader communicate to your people. Examine your climate. Does it hinder or encourage adaptation? Are you saying, by means of your policies, that you don't trust people to do the right thing without tight supervision? Do you stifle creativity and innovation by saying, in so many words, "This is the way we've always done it around here"? Does your compensation program reward or discourage adaptation?

How do you as a leader overcome these powerful barriers to adaptation? I believe that overcoming the resistance to adaptation and change involves three critical, fundamental, things: *mission*, *vision*, and *values*.

INSTILL THE MISSION

What is your organization about? Why is your product or service worth buying? Who *cares* about your organization, and why do they care? What do you collectively believe in? What's non-negotiable? Where are you going?

To answer these kinds of core questions, we need to look at mission, vision, and values.

Mission is your company's reason to exist. It's who you are, what you do, and why you do it. It's what makes you unique. It's why you've all agreed to work together to advance a common cause. Without a mission, you have no basis upon which to formulate your vision.

In a healthy organization, all key decisions are put through the screen of the mission. If a proposed tactic or strategy is not in keeping with the mission, you don't do it—period. The mission is the standard against which everyone's actions are judged.

Unfortunately, this is easier said than done. Judging a proposed action against the potential dollars-and-cents, bottom-line impact of that action is a tough enough challenge; judging such an action against a set of nonfinancial principles is even tougher. There are no easy answers, except to say that the mission must be clearly stated and that everyone in the organization must be prepared and willing to assess actions against the mission.

LOMBARDI RULE #3

Use your mission.
Define the goal. Pursue the goal.

Sometimes the mission can be threatening to a leader: Total commitment to the mission means that there are real limits on the leader's authority. If the leader issues orders that circumvent or contravene the mission, the members of the organization are obligated to protect the mission against the leader. (Again, this is easier said than done.)

The Green Bay Packers' mission could be boiled down to a succinct sentence: "Winning isn't everything; it's the only thing." I'll have more to say about this mission statement in Chapter 9, when I discuss my father's attitudes toward winning and losing. Everything the Packers did was judged against this mission: If the proposed action didn't contribute to winning, it wasn't done.

In the fall of 1962, during the height of the Cuban Missile Crisis, our country's leaders made a series of nonnegotiable demands and set a number of deadlines that our adversaries in the Soviet Union had to meet—or else. The "or else," everyone knew, was likely to be thermonuclear war. The nation was in a high state of anxiety, to say the least.

One of these deadlines happened to coincide with a Packer practice session. Someone approached my father and suggested that it might make sense to postpone the practice.

"To hell with Cuba," Lombardi replied flatly. "Let's go to work!"

In 1969, during my father's all-too-brief stint with the Washington Redskins, someone asked him if practice could be postponed for a half hour so that the team could watch the Apollo astronauts blast off on their historic mission to the moon. No, Lombardi replied; it wouldn't help either the Redskins or the astronauts to delay practice. He then gave a short inspirational talk about courage and commitment and invited the entire team to kneel and say a prayer for the Apollo team. Then practice began.

"We had some practice," a player said later that day.

SHAPE AND SHARE THE VISION

Vision is more practical than mission. Vision translates the mission into a concrete plan for results. It describes the future you seek to create. It is short and succinct.

Vision is a story communicated by symbols, analogies, and metaphors. Good leaders are good storytellers, and that skill is critically important in the rendering of the vision. A good vision is a story that gets people excited about bringing it to a successful conclusion. The leader identifies the challenges that lie between the vision and the way things are today, focusing everyone's attention on the challenges, while still painting a picture of the successful end of the story.

Visions take place in a human context. It's a reality of life that people and organizations *slow down* in the face of change. Consciously or unconsciously, they start dragging their feet. Psychologists tell us that planned change is far scarier than unplanned change. It's like scheduling a root canal: You have a whole lot of time to worry about (and exaggerate) the impending trauma.

By definition, visions are all about planned adaptation to change. If the vision-directed change is perceived as threatening, people begin shifting their loyalty from the organization to themselves. At that point, the vision can be more of a negative than a positive.

Retaining people's loyalty is why good leaders involve all members of the organization in creating, articulating, and communicating the vision. Good leaders share the vision-creating task, to broaden the base of ownership, generate commitment, and reduce the level of threat inherent in the planned adaptation to change.

Since all changes carry a price tag, leaders must give people a compelling reason to put forth their best effort. This can be a twofold approach: challenge and reward. Leaders keep people challenged by giving them responsibility and a chance to contribute to the vision. People's commitment increases when they feel necessary—when they see a clear connection between their individual effort and accomplishing the vision. And in terms of reward, people will put more in if they stand to get more out. They must be able to see a meaningful link between their effort and pain, on the one hand, and rewards, on the other. If the change generates financial rewards, those rewards must be shared. Victories should be celebrated, and recognition should be granted freely and often.

> *To win, the team must somehow get the feeling*
> *that there is dedication coming from the top.*

The premise for the vision ought to be: *We can do better.* In other words, the fuel for realizing the vision has to be optimism. Leaders must be enthusiastic and proactive, all the time communicating, communicating, and communicating the vision. Getting the message out is a constant, never-ending task. You need to be out and about, soliciting ideas, speaking to people's concerns, and enthusiastically selling the vision. You may vary the medium and the venue, but you don't vary the message. It's short, succinct, repeated often, and backed up by action. Sooner or later, people begin to believe you mean it.

LOMBARDI RULE #4

Create a shared vision.
"We can do better" is a good place to start.

In Chapter 5, we talked about sacrifice and total commitment on a personal level: the decision to choose one path over another, with the awareness that it means giving things up. Individuals do this only when they have a clear sense of the goal: the championship, the big contract, victory in the election.

This challenge is even greater at the organizational level. As we said earlier, if people can't *see* it, they can't commit to it. Unless your power to articulate a vision is strong, you can't call forth organizational commitment. Your people have to see, hear, taste, and smell the vision. They have to recognize it when it comes down the hall.

During Lombardi's second year in Green Bay, the Packers lost the 1960 championship game to the Philadelphia Eagles. The game was played in Philadelphia the day after Christmas. The Packers outplayed the Eagles, but came up short on the scoreboard, losing 17–13. It was a devastating defeat for the Packers, who left the field knowing they were the better team.

My father quickly called the players together in the locker room. Without yelling, or even raising his voice, he made a powerful, vision-rich speech: "Perhaps you didn't realize that you could have won this game. But I think there's no doubt in your minds now. *And that's why you will win it all next year.*" Jim Ringo, the All-Pro center on that team, recalled him saying, "We are men, and we will never let this happen again. We will never be defeated in a championship game again. Now we can start preparing for next year."

We will never be defeated in a championship game again. The Packers won the NFL championship the following year—and the year after that, for good measure.

Visions change. The vision that earns you your first championship may not secure you a fourth or fifth championship. The leader must constantly assess how the established vision fits in with the organization's evolving needs and, when necessary, begin a process of recalibration.

My father knew that the 1967 season would be a particularly difficult one for the Packers. They were the oldest team in the NFL. They'd just won their second consecutive championship and their fourth in six years. From that point on, every team they played would be gunning for them, since every team in the league set their sights on accomplishing one goal: beating the two-time champs!

Lombardi knew he needed something to rekindle the desire in his veterans to push for a third championship. From the first day of that 1967 training camp, therefore, he held up a new vision in front of the team: *a third championship.* This was their "challenge," he told them. No team had ever won three in a row, he said; maybe none ever would. (And as of this writing, no other team has.) But this year, he said passionately, *"we have that chance!"*

The championship ring that the Packers earned at the end of that season by beating the Oakland Raiders has three diamonds across its face, representing the three consecutive championships. And on one side of the ring is the word CHALLENGE.

When creating your vision, you must look beyond current reality. Don't make the mistake of limiting your vision by what seems possible today. If you do, you will confine your vision to what appears to be realistic—and where is the inspiration to be found in that?

IDENTIFY AND LIVE YOUR VALUES

A third concept—*values*—speaks to how you and your people intend to conduct yourselves as you pursue your vision.

> *The objective is to win: fairly, squarely, decently, win by the rules, but still win.*

Values are the way people actually do things. Your agreed-upon values determine the behaviors within your culture. Like mission and vision, your values are non-negotiable. They get to issues of *professionalism*, in the literal sense of "professing" things. In his first meeting with the Packer players, for example, Lombardi told them, "You may not be a football player. You may not be a tackle. You may not be a guard. You may not be a back. But you *will* be a professional."

Values come in two forms: *espoused* and *practiced*. The leader's challenge is to bring the two into alignment. Failure to do so leads to organizational cynicism—*we say it, but we sure don't do it!*—and eventually undercuts the leader's moral authority and credibility.

LOMBARDI RULE #5

> ### Align your values.
> Bring espoused values into congruence with practices—or else!

The way to work toward alignment is for the leader to ask some tough questions and see where the organization comes down on them. Is there a difference between what we say we believe and what we actually do when the pressure is on?

Here are some good (i.e., tough) questions:

- How do we spend our time?
- How do our values square with our calendar?
- How do we spend our money?
- How do we react in a crisis?
- What do we measure?
- What do we reward?
- What do we punish?
- Do we practice what we preach?
  - If we say we value teamwork, how do we handle that brilliant performer who seems to work best alone (the "solo artist")?
  - If we say we value openness, how do we treat the bearer of bad news?

The Packers of the 1960s had a nearly exact congruence between their espoused values and their practiced values, a circumstance that every leader hopes and prays for. The team's values were an extension of my father's values, and, as I noted in the introduction to this book, my father's values were sharply profiled and distinctive. He coached during the 1960s, a period in our nation's history when the things he so clearly stood for—sacrifice, discipline, and the dogged pursuit of excellence—were being widely questioned and often repudiated. The media focused their attention on the counterculture, Haight–Ashbury, and the increasingly troubling morass of Vietnam. My father's values stood out all the more as time passed. He became a symbol. Some people applauded him; many others attacked him.

Publicly, he put on a brave face:

Each of us must be prepared to adhere
to his principles, if he is certain in his own
conscience that he is doing right, if he is getting
the job done to his satisfaction and to the
approbation of the various publics he serves.
He must develop a thick skin to criticism
and let the caustic comments he receives
from some quarters pass over his head. It is
sometimes a hard thing to do, by the way—to go
out and even laugh at things that offend
sensibilities or offend families.

Privately, though, the criticisms stung. He hated having his friends and family read condemnations of "Vince Lombardi" in the newspapers or hear him vilified on television. (I put his name in quotes because our family barely recognized the person who was being cast in such a negative light.) To his credit, though, he never wavered. He had to live his values, and both he and his organization had to be viewed as driven by values. People could take exception to particular values embodied by the coach or the team, but they must never be given the opportunity to call the organization morally bankrupt.

Morally, the life of the organization must be of
exemplary nature. This is one phase where the
organization must not have criticism.

To that extent, at least, he succeeded. True, people were free to object to what they thought the Packers stood for. But in doing this, they acknowledged that the Packers did, indeed, stand for something. And in a relativistic age, that stood out.

I think it's worth noting for the record that my father was neither as dogmatic or "right-wing" in his values as his detractors sometimes made him out to be. He was conservative on some political issues, but quite liberal on many social issues. Many of the right-wing individuals and groups who wanted to embrace him as their own were scared off by his strong support of gun control—which he fervently supported in the wake of the Kennedy and King assassinations—and certain kinds of welfare, which he endorsed as part of our obligation to love each other.

Even the student protesters who came in for criticism from my father got a hearing of sorts. "We've got the young radicals who are throwing bombs at property," he said to a newspaper reporter, "and we've got radicals on the other side who don't want anybody to talk. Neither of them is worth a damn."

Sounds plenty tough, right? But he had more to say. "You hear the expression that this is the 'now generation,'" he said to another reporter, "but I don't think that's quite the right interpretation. I would call it the *why* generation. They don't want a yes or no. They're asking why. We can't have them defying authority on such places as campuses, but that's not the whole story. They're raising some questions that aren't being answered."

I think these are values in action. My father's approach to coaching, as noted in earlier chapters, emphasized the *why* of things. (Football players couldn't do their jobs if they didn't understand their job.) When Lombardi looked across the landscape of student protest in the late 1960s, he saw things that he disliked intensely. At the same time, he drew on his values to reach a deeper insight into the protesters. Weren't they, like his players, entitled to answers to their questions?

DEMONSTRATE COMPETENCE

People who are in trouble, who are feeling rudderless, are inclined to cut a new leader some slack. But the honeymoon lasts only so long. During that honeymoon, the leader must demonstrate his or her unquestioned competence.

By all accounts, Vince Lombardi knew his stuff. Pat Summerall, who later became an outstanding television color commentator, joined the Giants as a placekicker when my father was an assistant coach with that team. He remembers going to a training camp in Salem, Oregon, in 1958 and running into Vince Lombardi for the first time. Summerall was sitting in a meeting and started watching this compact, demonstrative assistant coach. In short order, he found himself asking, "Who the hell *is* that guy?"

"The guy had such an obvious complete command of what he was saying," Summerall recalls, "and he had everything down to how long the first step ought to be, how deep the guards ought to pull, and, you know, everything like that. It was Lombardi. . . . He knew every part of the machine, what the ends were supposed to do, what blocks the tackles and guards ought to call. Just a complete command of what he was teaching."

He made the same impression upon his arrival in Green Bay: *He knew every part of the machine.* "It was amazing," recalls assistant coach Jerry Burns. "That's the only way to describe it. He would study the film, then go to an owners' committee meeting at 11 o'clock, talk there for two hours, and then come back to us at 1 o'clock and tell us exactly how it was going to be in the next game."

LOMBARDI RULE #6

Know your stuff.
When the time comes, show that you know it.

I've already referred several times to my father's long apprenticeship: high school, Fordham, West Point, and New York. He chafed at being an assistant for so many years and resented being held back. But over all those years, he also achieved a level of mastery over his craft that few others ever attained. This mastery served him well when he finally got his opportunity. Coaches and players alike understood that Lombardi was unlikely to make naïve mistakes. Because he was so clearly competent, the occasional bad call or bad break never undercut his authority.

And finally, of course, the team began to *win*. Winning in football reflects the convergence of a lot of people's competence. But just as the leader is held primarily accountable for losses, he or she is also held primarily responsible for wins that are achieved on the field by others.

A leader is judged in terms of what others do to obtain the results that he is placed there to get.

BUILD CONFIDENCE

A man who is trained to his capacity will gain confidence. Confidence is contagious and so is lack of confidence and a customer will recognize both.

Confidence means trusting in someone and relying upon them. Interestingly enough, it also means relying on oneself—self-reliance.

In the three years before my father arrived in Green Bay, the Packers' win–loss records were 4–8, 3–9, and 1–10–1. All the momentum, in other words, was in the wrong direction. Confidence would have been hard to find anywhere in the vicinity of Lambeau Field. Then something unexpected happened: In came a new coach, who stated flatly that he had never been part of a losing team and sure didn't intend to start now.

You defeat defeatism with confidence.

When the Packers won the first Super Bowl, the 22 starters on offense and defense came from 22 different colleges. Not one had played on a national collegiate championship team. Only one was a first-team All-American in college. Only two were first-round draft choices. Only three had won a major bowl game in college. Players came from schools like Philander Smith and Valparaiso, not exactly football powerhouses. One player was drafted in the 11th round of the pro draft; others went in the 13th, 17th, and 20th rounds. One wasn't drafted at all.

So how can we explain the success the Packers enjoyed in the 1960s? If I had to pick a one-word summary, I'd pick the word *confidence.*

When Bart Starr, the All-Pro quarterback during Lombardi's years in Green Bay, attended his first meeting with his new coach, he was overwhelmed by the level of planning and preparation that Lombardi brought to the meeting. At the first break, he rushed to the phone to call his wife. "We're going to win," he told her excitedly.

That was exactly the impression that Lombardi was trying to create, and he was clearly successful. Out of the team's earshot, however, he was far less optimistic. After studying Packer films upon his arrival in Green Bay, he confessed his own doubts to his secretary, Ruth McKloskey. "I think I have taken on more than I can handle," he confided. "Will you pray for me and help me?" But no word of these doubts ever crept into the locker room or out onto the field.

What set Coach Lombardi apart was his ability to make each player feel confident and believe in himself. My father practically *oozed* confidence—in the forcefulness of his voice, his carriage, his very presence. He once said that you dispel defeatism by "grabbing it by the ears and throwing it out."

> ### *I am not going before that ball club without being able to exude confidence.*

Projecting confidence was partly stage setting, of course. The real confidence builder was *preparation.* Lombardi prepared his players for every game, for every eventuality. Going into a game, they believed they would never encounter a situation they weren't prepared to handle. What was Julius Caesar's celebrated analysis of his legions? "Without training, they lacked knowledge. Without knowledge, they lacked confidence. Without confidence, they lacked victory."

We are going to win some games. Do you know why? Because you are going to have confidence in me and my system.

Red Smith, the legendary sportswriter, once said that Lombardi's Packers were the smartest, most articulate athletes he had ever covered. In part, this reflected the quality of the players Lombardi chose to be Packers. But it was also a direct result of *preparation*. Every play was explained thoroughly from each player's perspective: why it should be run a certain way and how the defense would react to the play. This was no small task: Lombardi's passing attack (for example) was the most sophisticated in the game in the '60s. He was one of the first coaches to teach his quarterback and receivers to read the defense and react accordingly.

My father believed that preparation for a football game was 80 percent physical and 20 percent mental. This ratio, he also believed, reversed during the competition itself. At that stage, it was 80 percent mental and 20 percent physical. Football was a "game played above the shoulders," he often said, which meant that you needed confidence, which meant in turn that you needed to be completely prepared.

To play with confidence, a team must feel that everything possible has been done to prepare it fully for the coming game, and there is nothing more we can tell them.

Coach Lombardi didn't tolerate errors—particularly mental errors—that showed a lack of preparation on the players' part. If you made a lot of mental errors, you eventually found yourself playing somewhere else. And because only the relatively mistake-free players endured, the team as a whole gained confidence that it would never beat itself. A game in 1962 is a good example. Playing the Detroit Lions in Green Bay, the game turned into a fierce defensive struggle. With less than a minute to play, the Packers were behind 7–6. The Lions had the ball. A running play and a punt would seal the win for them. Inexplicably, the Lions' quarterback threw a pass, Herb Adderley intercepted, Paul Hornung kicked a field goal, and Green Bay won a game a less confident team would have expected to lose and would have lost.

A team that thinks it's going to lose is going to lose.

Lombardi used the rhythm of the week, from Tuesday through Sunday, as a long process of confidence building. On Tuesday, in the wake of a game, Lombardi could be very negative as he watched game films from the preceding Sunday. Players learned to dread these sessions if the Sunday game hadn't gone well. The veterans among them, though, knew that there was an enormous difference between a losing game played badly and a losing game played hard and well. After a hard-fought loss, Lombardi didn't run down his players; he knew they already felt bad enough.

After Tuesday, Lombardi would revert almost exclusively to positive comments and advice.

As soon as error is corrected, it is important that the error be forgotten and only the successful attempts be remembered. Errors, mistakes, and humiliations are all necessary steps in the learning process. Once they have served their purpose, they should be forgotten. If we constantly dwell

> *upon the errors, then the error or failure*
> *becomes the goal.*

For the rest of the week, the coach built up his players' self-image and confidence. He told them *how* they could win and, thereby, increased their belief in that outcome. "We were trained to win," Green Bay linebacker Dan Currie once commented. "The whole psychology was aimed that way. We got confidence and spirit, and we did win."

LOMBARDI RULE #7

Generate confidence.
Set the stage psychologically, and give people
the tools they need.

For instance, Lombardi rarely talked about injuries. His explanation was insightful. "If you were with the Packers and were a sub," he once asked rhetorically, "and if you read in the paper on Thursday that I had suggested that we were going to lose because the 'regular' was unable to play because of injuries, how would you feel? If I suggested we were going to lose because you were going to play, you would not feel very confident in yourself."

Success, in turn, brought more confidence, which brought more success. "You'd be surprised," my father liked to say, "how much confidence a little success will bring."

A great deal of that confidence originated from, and was invested in, the person of Vince Lombardi. Halfback Paul Hornung, who knew my father better than most players, was a believer. "If Lombardi told me to move out wide on the next play, jump over the wall, run into the stands, and buy a program," Hornung once said, "I would have thought it had some direct bearing on the play. It might even score a touchdown."

My father's players believed in him. Because of that, they also came to believe in *themselves*. After all, that's who *he* believed in.

His system, his success, was built on the premise that the players could do what he demanded of them. He asked them to have confidence in him and his system, and together they would succeed.

You've got to be sensitive to the needs of others.
And in return, the attitude toward you would be,
should be, one of confidence.

INSIST ON EXCELLENCE

You owe something to these people who are
coming to see you today. When this game ends, I
want them to say they just saw the greatest team
they ever saw. They just saw the greatest defensive
end they ever saw. They just saw the greatest
offensive guard they ever saw. If they don't come
out saying that, your record doesn't mean anything.

The word "excellence" comes from Latin words that mean "to rise out of." So excellence is the state of superior performance "rising out of" an original state of potential.

My father insisted on excellence up and down the Packer organization and in every aspect of the team's on-field performance. He believed that people wanted to excel: "That's a human constant," he once said. He understood the importance of setting extremely high standards and never relaxed those standards.

If you settle for nothing less than your best, you
will be amazed at what you can accomplish in
your life.

Quarterback Bart Starr understood why Lombardi pushed so hard on excellence. "Your consistent unwillingness to settle for anything less than excellence," he once wrote to my father, "will always serve as an inspirational beacon for all of us who played for you."

Leaders have to choose *how* their organizations will pursue excellence. There are many models to pick from, or use in combination. One is the *competitive victory model*. This is a zero-sum game: I win; you lose. To achieve this kind of excellence, you must beat your competitors; you must rise above the crowd. In one sense, the kind of gamesmanship that the competitive model encourages will bring out the best in people, as they stretch themselves to their limits to beat the competition. In other words, it's a *pushing* motivation. You push the competition; they push you.

The risk in this model, of course, is that it encourages an individualistic, adversarial attitude, which can be poisonous if you are trying to create a cooperative, team-based atmosphere. As David Sarnoff once said, "Competition brings out the best in products and the worst in people."

Coach Lombardi subscribed to this motivation nowhere more clearly than when he described the NFL "runner-up" bowl for second-place teams, a game the Packers played in following the 1963 and 1964 seasons. He called it a "game for losers played by losers."

The *comparative growth model* moves you in the direction of excellence by comparing your current condition to the way you were in the past. You see this model at play in the Olympic games. There are winners and losers, of course, but most Olympic athletes are seeking to achieve their personal best. Are you closer to your goal today than you were yesterday? Are you improving? Here you need a vivid, precise vision of your best, an honest picture of where you are today, a strategy to achieve your vision, and accurate benchmarks to gauge your progress. This model exerts a pulling motivation, in the sense that the goal—to be your best—pulls you toward itself. Used as an exclusive mind-set, it encourages a narrow self-focus and self-absorption, which can be fatal to an organization engaged in a competitive environment.

The *collaborative growth model* depends on the extensive use of partners and teams. You are seeking synergy with others that wouldn't otherwise be possible. The proverbial "whole that is bigger than the sum of the parts" is more than just a multiple of how many people are participating. This model creates a *supportive* motivation: You encourage one another; you are motivated to not let your teammates down.

LOMBARDI RULE #8

Chase perfection.
Settle for excellence along the way.

The fourth dimension that determines success or failure is selfless teamwork and collective pride, which accumulate until they make positive thinking and victory habitual.

My father employed all three of these models, although he certainly never learned or used the jargon of contemporary organizational theory. He understood that some people, the great ones, are self-motivated to be their best. Others are motivated by the goal of beating the competition. Still others take their greatest satisfaction from being a part of a successful team effort. His task, and the task of every leader, was to determine what motivated each individual. Not everyone responds the same way. The leader must find each person's "hot button."

Jerry Kramer, the all-pro guard who threw the critical block in the 1967 championship game, tells of an incident that occurred early in his career. During a goal-line scrimmage, Jerry couldn't seem to do anything right; he was jumping offside, missing his assignments. My father got in Kramer's face. "Mister," he yelled, "the attention span for a grade school kid is 30 seconds, for a high school kid a minute, for a college kid three minutes! Mister, where does that leave you?" He called him a "fat cow," as well as a bunch of other things I can't repeat.

By the end of practice, Kramer was ready to quit—*seriously* ready to quit. (Clearly, at least on this occasion, Lombardi had failed to find Jerry's "hot button.") Kramer later recalled that he was sitting in front of his locker trying to decide whether to quit immediately or wait until the end of the season. Lombardi walked through the locker room, took a look at Kramer, and sized up the situation. He walked over, tousled Kramer's hair, and told him, "Son, someday you are going to be one of the greatest guards in football."

Kramer will tell you that from that day forward, he never had to be pushed as a football player. He will tell you that from that point on, his sole motivation as a football player was, "I want to be, one of the greatest guards in football." On the second attempt, Coach Lombardi found his guard's "hot button."

Lombardi believed strongly in the benefits of competition; indeed, he thought that it was a bedrock of the American economy and culture. He encouraged individuals and teams to be better than they were last year or last week. And he placed an extraordinary emphasis on the value of teamwork and on creating success as a group that could not be achieved by individuals.

Football, like every other field of endeavor, has its elite, and this elite is based on excellence in execution. Excellence is achieved by the relentless pursuit of perfection. Lombardi talked as often about perfection as he did about excellence. He considered excellence to be an attainable by-product of the quest for perfection, which even he admitted was not attainable. He thought of the quest for perfection, whether as a coach or a player, as both necessary and frustrating. "The satisfactions are few, I guess, for perfectionists," he once wrote, "but I have never known a good coach who wasn't one."

No one is perfect, but boys making the effort to be
perfect...is what life is all about.

*The closer you get to the goal line, the more crucial
the situation, the more perfect you should be.*

LEARN FROM ADVERSITY

*"How does a man meet his failures?" my father
once asked rhetorically. "That is the measure of the
man. If he does not quit or curl up, he has the
right stuff in him. Be a hard loser."*

In Chapter 5, I talked at some length about the importance of mental toughness, a "winning habit" that enables the leader as an individual to ride out the inevitable setbacks and bumps in the road.

In this context—teaching and coaching—I want to make a few of the same points from a team perspective.

My father wanted a team of players who got stronger and gained resolve when they lost. He wanted people around him who found ways to grow in defeat.

*The real glory is in being knocked to your knees
and then coming back. We just have to button up
our pride, and we will come back.*

He knew that such players were a rare commodity and that he probably would never find enough of them to make up a complete football team. But if he could assemble a handful of people who could react to adversity that way—who could "use defeat as a stimulus to tougher effort"—that would be the core of a magnificent football team. "You never find forty men who feel that way," he once said, "but I'll take all I can get."

One last point: My father steadfastly refused to admit that the Packers were ever beaten. "When we lost a ball game," he said on many occasions, "it [was] only because time ran out on us."

Chuck Mercein, a fullback who played for my father in both Green Bay and Washington, made much of this notion. "He refuses to accept defeat," he once said, "even when he is defeated. I think he really believes that if the game goes on for another five minutes, he can win. It makes a difference to play under a guy like that, I can tell you."

Obviously, the coach doesn't want a team that has just turned in a losing effort to walk home with its tail between its legs. But I think there was something more to my father's attitude than simple spin-control. I think he was giving a strong message to his players about dealing with adversity: *What would we have done differently if the game had gone on another five minutes? How would we have turned it around? What should we do next time?*

LOMBARDI ON TEACHING AND COACHING

My father often used the words "teaching" and "coaching" interchangeably. He was the coach of the Green Bay Packers; he was the teacher of the Green Bay Packers. He was a "molder" of men, which applies equally to teachers and coaches.

> *To be the coach of a great football team, you've got to be a good teacher. "Molder" might be a better word. The team must be molded into a unit, must have a character absolutely of its own, without, in any way, affecting the enormous value of personal aggressiveness of pride.*

As both a teacher and a coach, Lombardi concentrated on the *whys*. "I never tell a player, 'This is my way, now do it,'" he once said. "Instead, I say, 'This is the way we do it, and this is why we do it.'"

Lombardi taught as he had taught many years before to his students at St. Cecilia's. He taught to the bottom of the "class," going slowly enough and being repetitive enough so that no one was left behind. The rationale was simple: If somebody doesn't get the point of the lesson and makes a mistake in the game, the efforts of 10 other people can be instantly negated. And in Lombardi's model of football, every man was required to think for himself. Coaches can find ways to cover up a player's physical shortcomings; they can't cover for their mental mistakes during the course of a game.

"Vin was a great teacher," Giants owner Wellington Mara once commented. "He could get on a blackboard and hammer into the lower portion of the mentality. [Tom] Landry would not do that. He would know that there were only three or four people in the room who knew exactly what he was saying."

> *We are showing them the Lions' game of last Sunday against the Colts, stopping the projector and running it back again and again so that they will know the reasoning behind our thinking, behind what we are putting in for this game and what we are asking them to do.*

> *They call it coaching, but it is teaching. You do not just tell them it is so, but you show them the reasons why it is so and you repeat and repeat until they are convinced, until they know. It was the way, back in Brooklyn, the good teachers I had and admired did it.*

The risk in this style of teaching/coaching, of course, is that the top of the class—or even the teacher—will get bored. Lombardi avoided this eventuality in part by the simple force of his personality and convictions. He had a way of making even a routine task sound important, as if there were *no* routine tasks. Like West Point's Red Blaik, he had a gift for making complicated things sound simple. This, too, made mundane things into compelling things. Practice sessions that might have been deadly in the hands of a less gifted teacher remained interesting, even in their umpteenth repetition. "I loved it," recalled Bart Starr. "I loved the meetings. I never, ever was bored or tired at any meeting we were in with Lombardi. I appreciated what he was trying to teach. He was always trying to raise the bar."

Lombardi's next quarterback, Sonny Jurgenson, was even more succinct: "He was a great teacher," he said of his coach.

LOMBARDI RULE #9

> **Live what you teach.**
> And live what you coach. And sell what you teach and coach.

Great teachers (and great coaches) win the hearts of their students. They do so, Lombardi used to say, by *selling* themselves—being "involved right up to your neck" and making that commitment clear. "You've got to live it all day long," he once commented, "in the car, at home, at night, looking at the pictures, out on the practice field."

In other words, Lombardi was also a *salesman*. He sold himself to the team and the team to itself.

> *Coaching is selling. Selling is teaching. My customers are not so much the fans, but rather the players. I have to first sell them on themselves, and then on the small hurts, because the small hurts are not only a part of football, but also a part of life. And then I must sell them on this team, on this season, on this game, and each individual play as the most important thing in their lives.*

Pat Fischer, defensive back for the Redskins, developed a clear insight into Lombardi's teaching and coaching techniques.

"Lombardi is a salesman," he said. "He has to sell us on winning. Each day he sells the team. He's leading up to the right moment to clinch the sale, and that's supposed to be on Sunday. That's the day we buy. He always tries to close the sale on Sunday. Sometimes he does, and sometimes he doesn't. It's hard to sell forty men week after week. . . . I have the feeling that each day, Lombardi tries to think of some little story or parable he might tell that will stick in your mind all week, make you susceptible for the Sunday sale, sort of like a car salesman pointing out a new accessory every day. Lombardi's all design."

I'm pretty sure that "car salesman" was not the image that my father was hoping to create in the minds of the Redskins. And to be fair to him, he had only one season with that team to bring them around to his way of thinking—and to put together a team with players who subscribed to his way of thinking. But Fischer's notion of the coach pacing himself, and pacing the "client," toward the "closing of the deal" on Sunday was exactly right. And Lombardi was a master at closing the deal.

STRIKE THE BALANCE: CAMARADERIE AND DISTANCE

*The leader can never close the gap between himself
and the group. If he does, he is no longer what he
must be. He must walk a tightrope between the
consent he must win and the control he must exert.*

As you climb the ranks of the organizational hierarchy, the demands that the organization places upon you change in many ways, some obvious and some subtle. New titles, of course, bring new responsibilities, a broader perspective, more direct reports. These are the obvious changes. But new titles also bring, among other things, a change in the relationship between the leader and the led.

When my father was with the Giants and still an assistant coach, he played golf with the players in the daytime and cards with them at night. Sometimes he had players over to our house for dinner. One time, just before the regular season began, he decided that the team was too tense. While head coach Jim Lee Howell was out of town, my father threw a party for the entire team. He wouldn't have claimed cause and effect, of course, but the team did loosen up and did go on to win the division championship that year.

In Green Bay, Lombardi kept his distance from the players. Now he played golf and cards with friends from the local business community. He didn't socialize with his assistants. He was the *leader*.

This was a turn of events that my father wasn't particularly happy about. One of the things he liked best about football was the close association with the players, the camaraderie. As an assistant, he was able to enjoy that easy relationship to the fullest. Things changed when he became head coach. True, he was also getting older, and it would have been unrealistic to imagine that he could stay close to generations of football players who were getting progressively "younger." But he also knew that changed circumstances called for new behavior from Vince Lombardi.

> *Leaders are lonely people and, whether cordial or remote in manner, are destined to maintain a certain distance between themselves and the members of the group.*

When he referred to the leader as a "lonely person," he was including himself (as a head coach) in that group. He didn't like that loneliness, but took it to be an inevitable aspect of his job.

At the same time, however, he was still intimately involved in the lives of several dozen young men. He may have been "distant," but he was still in contact. The head coach had a thousand opportunities a day to keep an eye on his players. "They act like the brothers in an unselfish, rough family," wrote one sportswriter, and the person who created that family was Vince Lombardi.

All of this changed when he stepped down as Green Bay's head coach. Now he was a "leader"—in the sense of being a general manager—without the benefit of a coach's link to the lives of his players. It was a painful and abrupt transition, which he likened to losing a family. Eventually, his desire to recreate what he had lost led him to accept the Redskins' offer of the head coaching position:

> *There's a great closeness on a football team, you know—a rapport between the men and the coach that's like no other sport. It's a binding together, a knitting together. For me, it's like fathers and sons, and that's what I missed. I missed players coming up to me and saying, "Coach, I need some help because my baby's sick." Or, "Mr. Lombardi, I want to talk with you about trouble I'm having with my wife." That's what I missed most. The closeness.*

LOMBARDI RULE #10

Strike the balance.
Be as close as you can be—and as far away as you have to be.

I include the foregoing coda to make the point that when it comes to distance between leaders and followers, the standards become highly personal and individual. I think my father was right in arguing for a self-imposed distance between the leader and the led. But he also knew that a good leader *feels deeply* for his people— in fact, that's in the unwritten job description—and that these ties have to be acknowledged, too. They're part of the job—and part of being a caring human being.

THE LOMBARDI RULES

Teaching, coaching, and leading

Be authentic.
Act your integrity. Be predictable. Make amends when you foul up.

Earn trust through investment.
Use your authority to build the organization's trust in you.

Use your mission.
Define the goal. Pursue the goal.

Create a shared vision.
"We can do better" is a good place to start.

Align your values.
Bring espoused values into congruence with practices—or else!

Know your stuff.
When the time comes, show that you know it.

Generate confidence.
Set the stage psychologically, and give people the tools they need.

Chase perfection.
Settle for excellence along the way.

Live what you teach.
And live what you coach. And sell what you teach and coach.

Strike the balance.
Be as close as you can be—and as far away as you have to be.

Building the Winning Organization

For all who make it, there's got to be selflessness, a sublimation, automatically, of the individual to the whole.

Vince Lombardi is remembered as a *winner*. His championships with the Green Bay Packers and his career win–loss record set him apart from all other coaches in professional football. The enduring image—the one that winds up on the covers of most books about him—is being carried from the field on the shoulders of his jubilant players.

In the next few chapters, I will make the case that his outstanding record *on* the football field reflected the hard work that he did *off* the field. What Vince Lombardi was really about was building a winning organization, one that performed off the field as well as on the field. Over the next three chapters, I'll explain how he built that organization and how he maintained its winning edge. This involved setting up effective structures and an effective system and also recruiting good people and motivating them to work within that system.

PICKING THE WINNING JOB

Building the winning organization begins with an obvious, but critical, choice: *Which organization are you going to affiliate yourself with?*

Answering this question requires a careful reading of the marketplace. Even the most talented manager could fail by taking the right job at the wrong time. For example, going into almost any aspect of the real-estate business in 1990 would have been a bad bet. Similarly, in the fall of 2000, many of the high flying dot coms came falling back to earth after several years of incredible growth. As a result, thousands of workers and managers lost their jobs as companies were forced to cut back on their spending.

The ideal management job may be found in a situation that meets the following two criteria: (1) The ranks of the organization are full of latent talent that has yet to show itself, and (2) the organization itself is well positioned in an industry that's about to take off.

Those were the circumstances that prevailed in Green Bay, Wisconsin, in 1959. Very few people saw it that way, of course. The team's horrible 1958 record of 1–10–1 obscured some important facts. Thanks in large part to eight years of superb work by Jack Vainisi, the Packers' Director of Scouting —and also due to the high draft picks that resulted from a succession of miserable seasons—the Packers of the late 1950s were endowed with talent. But that talent had not gelled. Why? Mainly because the Green Bay coaches prior to Lombardi had proved unable to take these talented individuals and mold them into *a team*. Although many in the NFL did not see the Packers as competitive, others, including Vince Lombardi, saw opportunity in Green Bay.

Another thing that not everybody at the time understood was that professional football—the Packers' industry—was about to take off. College football had long been considered the pinnacle of the game. Its supposedly "amateur" players were seen as more noble than their professional counterparts, who were involved in "play for pay." But in the 1950s, some colleges began to de-emphasize football, feeling that it was too distracting, unnecessarily violent, too expensive, or simply not what an academic institution ought to be focusing its attention on.

But what would fill the void after some once-proud college football programs—including Fordham, Lombardi's own alma mater—left the field? Baseball may have been the "national pastime," but football had a distinctive appeal to a growing number of Americans. It was action, but it was also the *anticipation of action*, that made football fascinating. My father phrased it in an interesting way:

> **You know why football is so popular? Those people running around hitting each other? Hell, no. It's because of the huddle. Every time the clock stops, every time the play is over, the huddle forms, and the fan puts himself in the same situation, tries to figure out what he would do. Football is situation, as much as action.**

But could pro football, which had always been seen as an afterthought to the college game, win the hearts of Americans? The answer came at the end of the 1958 NFL season, when the Baltimore Colts and the New York Giants played a classic championship game. A battle of two great teams, punctuated by acts of great athleticism and courage, the game subsequently was dubbed "the greatest football game ever played." It was also the first NFL championship game that was played under the new "sudden-death" rules, which called for play beyond regulation time to break a tie. And coincidentally, the game was broadcast to a national TV audience, which was thrilled with what it saw that day at Yankee Stadium, as the Colts beat the Giants in overtime. Although the broadcast was crude by today's standards, it was clear that football and television were a good match. (Television got viewers closer to the action than they would have been in the stadium itself.) Large forces were converging.

My father was on the Giants sideline during that pivotal game, serving as the Giants' offensive coach. By then, of course, he was well established with the Giants as a successful and respected assistant coach. But that cut both ways. Longtime assistant coaches tended to retire as longtime assistant coaches. Lombardi, however, wasn't necessarily doomed to that fate if he stayed with the Giants.

The team's owners, Jack and Wellington Mara, seemed to have made an informal promise to my father that when Giant head coach Jim Lee Howell retired, Lombardi would get the call to succeed him.

But there was no hint that the call would come anytime soon, and my father wasn't getting any younger. Howell, ably supported by his two notable assistants (Lombardi on the offense, future Hall of Famer Tom Landry on the defense), was enhancing his own job security by leading the Giants to victory. Lombardi, meanwhile, was having trouble sharing the limelight with Howell and Landry. "Vince was the type person who needed to be in charge," Landry later commented, I think with more than a touch of understatement. Having a strong peer like Landry may have been irksome to my father, although he had enormous respect for Landry. "I guess it was inevitable that two strong men like Vince Lombardi and Tom Landry would be at odds," Howell recalled. "They were fussing all the time."

LOMBARDI RULE #1

Pick the right organization.

This isn't quite as obvious as it sounds. Where can you go where there's a lot of unrealized potential and where there's a rising tide?

When the Philadelphia Eagles made an overture to my father in 1957, the year before the Colts–Giants championship game described above, he was sorely tempted. Then 45 years old, he was already older than many head coaches in the NFL. He confided to friends that he was despairing of ever getting one of the top 12 jobs in professional football. If he turned down Philadelphia, would he ever get another call?

Eventually, he decided against taking the job with the Eagles. His friends and advisors, including Giants owners Jack and Wellington Mara, persuaded him that he wouldn't have enough authority or autonomy with the Eagles, whose broad ownership base made them badly fragmented.

Wait for the right opportunity, they counseled him—and it was good advice.

DEMAND AUTONOMY, RESPECT AUTHORITY

When Vince Lombardi took over as the coach in Green Bay in the early months of 1959, therefore, he was clearly focused on running his own show. The Packer organization had agreed to let him serve as both coach and general manager, effectively giving him complete operating control of the club.

> *There aren't any owners here. I'm the only man*
> *who makes the decisions.*

Lombardi had it half right: There were owners in Green Bay; they just weren't the equivalent of the all-powerful Giants' owners. The team was owned by a large number of local people who held shares in a non-dividend-paying, non-profit corporation, making the Packers the only true "community" franchise in the NFL. Their interests were represented by an executive committee which had the ultimate responsibility for running the team. The committee had the ability to vest operating authority in one individual, and, with a clear understanding that the future of the franchise was probably on the line, they had agreed to vest it in Vince Lombardi:

> *It had to be autonomy, a one-man deal, or it*
> *wouldn't have worked at all.*

At his first executive committee meeting in Green Bay, my father made what must have been a startling announcement to some:

*I want it understood that I'm in
complete command. I expect full cooperation
from you people, and you will get full cooperation
from me in return. You have my confidence,
and I want yours.*

Part of my father's strategy here was to nip in the bud some bad habits that had taken root in Green Bay. In previous years, players had discovered that if they knew someone on the executive committee, they could sometimes translate that connection into more playing time. In some cases, at least, an overly intrusive board member would instruct Coach Raymond "Scooter" McLean, Lombardi's predecessor, to play that particular player more. My father would not tolerate that.

*If I were coaching and someone else in the
organization were questioning me,
I couldn't take that.*

It wasn't just specific instances like this that my father wanted to stop; he also wanted to give himself sufficient flexibility to build a winning organization his way. He had waited many years for this opportunity, and he was brimming over with energy and ideas about how to move the Packers forward. (In that sense, being forced to wait a few extra years was a great advantage.) He didn't want to waste time playing politics with a meddling board. He didn't want to risk realizing only half his vision; he knew that in order to make a difference, it had to be all or nothing.

Besides, no one ever said my father lacked for an ego. Without a doubt, he enjoyed the notion that he would be controlling the team and calling the shots.

*You mean, a one-man operation sort of thing?
Yeah, I like that. That's one of the things that*

makes it interesting. It's a $5 million business, and there are very few positions that big where one man has so much say-so. Can put his own stamp on things. I like that.

LOMBARDI RULE #2

Demand autonomy.
What do you absolutely have to control, to make your job possible? If you can't get that degree of autonomy, you can't succeed.

I've included many of my father's thoughts on this subject because it seems clear to me that by striking the right deal up front, he gave himself enormous latitude to make changes on the scale, and of the scope, that he was contemplating. This was truly a case in which a business turnaround was needed. (It's hard to get much lower than 1–10–1!) The Packers' executive committee had consciously gone out and hired what would today be called a "turnaround artist." Lombardi had demanded, and the board had agreed to cede, sufficient authority to make things happen.

Of course, these are the specifics of a particular situation. I think the generalizations *behind* the specifics, however, are still meaningful: Develop a clear sense of the right opportunity. Understand your bargaining position. Bargain for *autonomy*, especially if you're planning big changes. Give yourself enough elbowroom to survive the inevitable missteps of the initial phase of your new situation.

I should also point out that my father was not demanding unchecked, unlimited authority for himself. That would have been unrealistic. Despite his carefully engineered autonomy, he still lived within two hierarchies: the Packer organization and the NFL. Although he sometimes had disagreements with representatives of both of these organizations, he usually followed the rules and conducted himself as a subordinate when such conduct was appropriate.

Respect authority.
If you're going to ask people to respect your authority, you'll
need to lead by example. Whatever hierarchy you're in—
assuming its authority is legitimate–deserves your respect.

Giving an example to the contrary will help make the point. Late in his career, when an official made a particularly bad call against the Redskins—"bad" as my father saw it, at least—he followed the offending referee into his dressing room at the end of the game to continue complaining about the call. This was clearly against league rules. Commissioner Pete Rozelle wrote Lombardi a strongly worded letter criticizing him for his behavior and expressing surprise that a head coach who was "so personally dedicated to authority and respect for order" would flout the rules to such an extent. Rozelle later said that, on the basis of Lombardi's chastened behavior in a subsequent meeting, he [Rozelle] was convinced that this pointed reprimand was far more effective than the usual fine would have been.

At another point in my father's career, a major press conference was scheduled on the eve of a championship game. Everyone showed up except the head coach of one of the competing teams: Vince Lombardi. NFL employees reached my father by phone at his nearby hotel. Lombardi said that since he hadn't been informed of the press conference and already had made other plans, he wouldn't be attending. Commissioner Rozelle got on the phone. After a very brief conversation, my father said he'd be right over.

At the end of the press conference, someone thanked Lombardi for changing his plans and attending. His response was telling:

You gotta remember one thing: If you're going to
exercise authority, you've got to respect it.

This was one of my father's most deeply held beliefs. It grew out of his seminary training, his education with the Jesuits, and his apprenticeship at West Point with Red Blaik. Legitimate authority deserves respect—all the more so if you represent authority.

THE SELECTIVE ART OF DELEGATION

In 1959, the Green Bay Packers were a relatively small organization, without much management depth and certainly without much of a hierarchy. There were three dozen players, several assistant coaches, some part-time scouts, and a small office staff in Green Bay (and a second small staff in Milwaukee, where the team played a number of its games). My father's insistence on serving as both coach and general manager may have made life easier for him at the outset, in the sense that there weren't any divided responsibilities, and Coach Lombardi didn't have to wonder or worry about what General Manager Lombardi was thinking and doing, but it also put the responsibility for *all* of the team's affairs squarely on his shoulders.

At first, this was just fine with him. In a 1961 interview, he explained his thinking to longtime friend and journalist Tim Cohane:

> *I think I'd be unhappy if I didn't have the added duties of Green Bay's general manager. Tickets, salaries, TV and radio contracts all pose headaches beyond the migraine of trying to win games, but I thrive on work. I'm restless, demanding, sometimes impatient and hot-tempered. For these characteristics, a full schedule is the best antidote.*

Without attempting to psychoanalyze his boss, Packer public-relations director Chuck Lane painted much the same picture regarding my father's degree of involvement in the day-to-day operations of the Packer organization. "He knew where every paper clip was," Lane once commented. "That's the kind of control he kept, from top to bottom. A lot of times I thought all these details really had to clutter his thinking, but that's the way he wanted it. He insisted on control of everything." Jerry Burns, an assistant coach for the Packers between 1965 and 1967, made the same point. According to Burns, nothing escaped the coach's attention. As an example, Burns recalls how Coach Lombardi went so far as to ask all the wives how their rooms were the week before a game in Los Angeles.

But Ockie Krueger, a West Point friend and associate of my father's who directed the Packers' Milwaukee operations and then served in a similar capacity with the Redskins, had a somewhat different perspective. "When the Packers split their league schedule with half the games in Milwaukee and half in Green Bay," Krueger recalls, "he gave me complete charge of the Milwaukee part of it. I was not new to sports, of course, but I was new to the NFL and going into a new job, certain things frighten you. So I called him in Green Bay and asked him a question about something. I must have called him at the wrong time, because he said, 'I thought you were gonna run things for me down there in Milwaukee.' I said, 'Thank you very much.' That was the last question I ever asked him in the eleven years I was associated with him."

The difference in these perspectives, of course, is that Lane and Burns were referring to matters directly related to the performance of the football team—or, "directly related," the way my father defined things—whereas Krueger was concerned primarily with Milwaukee ticket sales and other strictly business-related issues. I'm pretty sure Chuck Lane was exaggerating about the paper clips, but I know that Lombardi personally reviewed most of the press releases that Lane wrote. He even rewrote many of them, because he felt that everything that appeared in the newspapers would be read by both his players and the opposing players as well.

Despite my father's claim that he worried about business matters down to the last ticket sold, most things on that level fell into the category of "out of sight, out of mind." Part of that, of course, reflected the fact that he had a lot of confidence in Ockie Krueger. If it was a nonfootball matter and Vince Lombardi had a lot of confidence in you, he would pretty much leave you alone to run your part of the organization.

LOMBARDI RULE #4

Delegate the second-tier stuff.
Look for existing competence in the organization, and take full advantage of that competence.

As for delegating things related to football, my father had a simple policy: *He didn't.* He controlled his assistant coaches—especially his offensive assistants—far more thoroughly than most of his counterparts did. He used them primarily as sounding boards. They were not expected to discipline players. Lombardi wanted to be the only coach who exerted significant control over the players.

The resulting prescription seems self-evident: Figure out what you *must* control, and control that. Then identify noncritical operations (like Milwaukee ticket sales) where you already have strong help, and define them as somebody else's problem.

LOMBARDI RULE #5

Check your hat.
Is your own position evolving? If so, how should the changes be reflected in your job description and those of others around you? Again, your successes should let you give things up.

A less obvious extension of this principle would be to *look for ways to move things from the first category to the second category.* This is especially important if you're the kind of person—like my father—who was temperamentally inclined to consider everything critical, especially when he was tackling a new situation. Things evolve if you let them. Learn to unload.

And finally, *figure out which hat you really need to wear, and figure out how long you need to wear it.* The primary reason my father quit coaching the Packers after the 1968 season was that he was overwhelmed by his two jobs: coach and general manager. He gave up the more stressful of the two roles, the coaching job that put him on national TV every in-season Sunday as either a *winner* or a *loser.* He soon regretted that decision. He had given up the job that he loved, the stress notwithstanding, in favor of the job that he had initially taken to protect his operational authority.

PREPARING THE ORGANIZATION FOR VICTORY

An organization is its people. A football team is primarily its players and secondarily its coaches and front-office personnel. Sometimes, an incoming coach stepping into a losing situation engages in a large-scale housecleaning. Heads roll left and right. This not only cleans out deadwood—(as the theory goes), but also makes a strong symbolic point: Things are going to be different around here.

Lombardi was fundamentally a conservative man. Except in extreme circumstances, he didn't believe in radical departures. That having been said, my father didn't hesitate to use different strategies to suit different circumstances. Arriving in Green Bay, where expectations were relatively low and he had some time to build toward success, he more or less started from scratch, educating a staff of new assistants to coach his way. Later in his career, when he went to Washington, expectations were higher, and the time frame was shorter. In that case, he kept two assistants who understood the Redskins' strengths and weaknesses. He complemented these "carryovers" with some veteran coaches who understood his system. "It is unwise," he explained, "to walk into a new job with a complete new staff."

The most difficult part of a new job, Lombardi once commented, is to analyze and understand the personality of each player.

The two main things on a new job are
the personality analysis and a talent analysis.
The idea is to make sure that every player
is in his best position.

Achieving this is harder than it sounds. Coaches puzzled then, and still puzzle today, over how to deploy their players effectively. Sometimes, they came up with brilliant new combinations. Other times, they came up with dumb ideas.

LOMBARDI RULE #6

Be brilliant, but don't be stubborn about it.
Yes, your job is to bring new insights and turn
things around. But forcing a square peg into a round
hole doesn't get either job done.

My father came up with a few of the latter. Green Bay's first draft pick in 1961 was a talented running back from Michigan State named Herb Adderley. He had been drafted for his speed and his talent for open-field running. In pre-season practices, Lombardi and his staff discovered that Adderley had "good hands" and ran pass routes well. Lombardi decided that he would try to use him as a receiver. Lombardi and the assistants put Adderley through his paces as a flanker and then put him in a game, and (as my father later recalled) "nothing happened."

Why? In his bones, in his heart, Adderley saw himself as a defensive back. He simply couldn't get comfortable on offense. My father and his assistants were too committed to their "insight" to change directions. After switching to the defense, Adderley went on to become a Hall of Fame cornerback.

For a whole half season, I had been so stubborn
that I had been trying the impossible.

One goal of my father's "personality analysis" and "talent analysis" was to figure out what everyone's maximum effort was—what 100 percent was—and look for ways to push and pull people toward that level of effort. As noted earlier, my father reserved for himself the task of driving and motivating his players. (See Chapter 8 for an examination of his motivational techniques.) Imagine the difficulty of figuring out how to deploy a Herb Adderley, multiplied by 36—an impossible task! So, in a critical sense, my father was dependent on the wisdom of his assistant coaches, who were themselves skilled professionals. One of them, Phil Bengtson, was an assistant during Lombardi's entire tenure with the Packers and succeeded him as head coach when Lombardi stepped down.

Training camp, of course, was another mechanism designed to help the head coach in his sifting-and-sorting process.

We put tremendous pressure on the rookie
in training camp. Purposely. There's pressure
on the veterans, too, after a six-month holiday,
but at least you already know their strengths
and weaknesses. Some of them put on a little
weight and perhaps get a little lazy.
We know how to correct that.

We may have as many as 35 rookies report to
camp. Only 5 or 6 will be there at the end. And I
have about four weeks to make my decision as to
whether it's go or no-go. If he doesn't have the
ability or talent, it's easy. Yet, when he obviously
has ability, talent, and agility, everything about him
looks good, I still have to figure out how he will
react with 60,000 people screaming in his ear.

> **Import.**
> If there's someone out there who already knows your
> system and can help you survive the building or rebuilding
> period, grab him or her.

Another technique employed by my father to start piecing a winning organization together was to trade for players who already knew his system. Shortly after arriving in Green Bay, for example, he picked up safety Emlen Tunnell from the Giants. Tunnell was a savvy veteran who understood Lombardi's defensive philosophy and was able to serve as an informal defensive "captain" on the field while the rest of the defensive team got up to speed. Later, with the Redskins, Lombardi picked up Chuck Mercein, Bob Long, and Tom Brown, former Packers who understood his system and—more importantly—his methods.

Sometimes this practice annoyed veteran players, who didn't understand why Lombardi was bringing in outsiders to replace their teammates. Lombardi didn't worry about this kind of grumbling from the players. Both in Green Bay and in Washington, he needed strong allies quickly. In addition to that, he generally favored veterans over rookies. Unlike the talented rookie Herb Adderley (for example), veterans were known quantities, and they made fewer mistakes. My father thought that it was generally easier to spot underutilized talent within the pro ranks than to pull off a coup in the annual college draft—although, as coach and general manager, he certainly spent plenty of time worrying about the draft.

SKILL BUILDING: THE BEST-CONDITIONED WINS

So far, I've emphasized techniques for putting the right players in the right place, assessing current players, bringing in veterans, and making decisions about first-year players.

One of the first steps in building a winning team is skill building: making your current players better. Good leaders provide their people with what they lack, including training, information, confidence, and discipline. This was the reward for the enormous pressure that Lombardi put on his players: his absolute, unwavering commitment to making those players *better*. The other reward, of course, was *winning*.

In *Second Effort*, the very successful sales training film described in Chapter 1, my father re-created his opening-day speech to his players as they reassembled in training camp after the off-season.

> ***I'm going to ask you to work harder than
> you've ever worked before in your life,
> because the history of the National Football League
> proves that most games are won in the last two
> minutes of the first half, or the second half. And
> it's usually the team which is best conditioned
> which usually wins the game. I'm going to
> expect a 100 percent effort at all times.
> Anything less than that is not good enough.***

The first step in training camp, from my father's perspective, was physical conditioning. (This went along with relearning the fundamentals of football, building skills, and installing the offensive and defensive systems.) Players who were with the Packers for the first time—rookies and veterans from other teams—were stunned at the physical demands that my father placed on them in the preseason. Some players vanished after the first grueling day.

> ***Good physical condition is vital to success.***

By contrast, poor physical condition leads to fatigue. Fatigue was the subject of one of the legendary signs that adorned the walls of the Packers' locker room: *Fatigue makes cowards of us all.*

Build skills.

Today, people are demanding that organizations provide them
with portable skills—and you can't put big demands on people
before you define and provide the needed skills.

Training camp was also the place where veterans and rookies alike
learned to do their jobs better. For the most part, this meant doing
specific drills over, and over, and over again, until doing those drills
successfully became second nature. "Again!" my father would shout
after a poorly executed play. "Again!" It was tough, boring, painful,
and, in the short term, immensely unpleasant work. But it was also
the kind of hard work that led to long-term payoffs.

Tight end Gary Knafelc had the best one-liner regarding the
level of work and commitment that was required. "Lombardi
works you so hard," Knafelc once said, "that when he tells you to
go to hell, you look forward to the trip."

The harder you work, the harder it is to lose.

One reason Lombardi was able to extract the kind of effort he
did from his players was that they understood that, if anything, he
was making an even *greater* effort. True, he wasn't experiencing
the cuts, bruises, and other minor injuries that players were incur-
ring on the practice field every day. But he pushed himself to the
limit, just as he pushed them. He came early, stayed late, and never
took a day off. And just as he didn't allow his players to "dog it"
during practices, he never took it easy on himself. When he was
there, he was really *there*.

Let 'em see you sweat.

Why should they kill themselves for the organization if you don't?

"Maybe that's the key," Redskins' quarterback Sonny Jurgensen once commented. "He works harder than anyone, [and] wants us to do well. You have to respect a man like that. He's total."

As my father built skills, he also monitored attitudes. Generally, people's attitudes should improve along with their skills, especially after they have a couple of wins under their belts. When that didn't happen, and my father decided that the situation couldn't be salvaged, he moved quickly to get rid of the "bad apple."

> *I don't want any bad apples in my organization.*
> *I get one apple in the bushel over here, and the*
> *rest of them will start rotting, too.*

BUILDING TEAM SPIRIT

As noted in Chapter 4, my father was a religious man, yet he didn't consider a championship to be a sign of divine favor. Instead, he thought that a team of people working together with discipline, singleness of purpose, and a commitment to excellence could prevail, no matter how heavily the odds were stacked against them. Lombardi understood that teams, not individuals, win championships. No matter how talented you were, you first had to be a good teammate, with the team spirit of sacrifice, discipline, trust, and respect. Absent those qualities, no player played for Vince Lombardi for very long.

My father spoke of teamwork. I believe "team spirit" more accurately describes what he was constantly trying to create with the Packer players. My reason for saying this is that, contrary to popular opinion, when people work in groups, they often don't work as hard as when they are working on their own. Put another way, in a group effort, the whole frequently does not exceed the sum of the parts.

There are many reasons for this phenomenon. Perhaps people work less because they do not trust their teammates. Or maybe it's because they believe that they can have only an indirect impact on the performance of the group, with praise and blame being less contingent on individual performance. Or people may feel that they can "hide" in a group setting, thereby getting a free ride and "coasting" on the group effort.

Given these group dynamics, what Coach Lombardi created, and what every leader should strive to create, is "team spirit," *the individual pursuit of excellence within the team concept.* When people have team spirit, they want the team to succeed, and they will hold themselves—and everyone else on the team—personally accountable for pursuing individual excellence.

Team spirit, in the Lombardi philosophy, grows out of three interrelated elements:

- Common goals
- Complementary skills and abilities
- Mutual accountability

Common goals create drive and energy. Building consensus is one of the leader's primary challenges. Leaders do not give everyone a vote, but should give everyone a voice. Teams will commit to the goal if they participate in the decision-making process.

A team on which every player hungers for the same outcome is a motivated team, a team that wants to close the gap between what is and what can be. Put another way, motivation comes from the gap that exists between the way things are and the way an individual or a team wants them to be. Common goals foster the subordination of the individual will to the group will.

> *Each man must contribute to the spirit—and this spirit is really the cohesive force that binds 11 hardened and talented men into a cohesive force. Just as you must contribute to the spirit of your company, to the spirit of your associates.*

Bart Starr offers an insider's perspective: "Lombardi explained that some of the players on the team were going to be famous, some obscure, but everyone was equally important. For us to succeed, we had to place our personal goals behind those of the team. We had to pick each other up and push each other to higher levels."

LOMBARDI RULE #10

> **Build team spirit.**
> This means common goals, complementary skills
> and abilities, and mutual accountability.

Complementary skills and abilities, of course, are what make football a great game. People play (and watch) football to experience the unique thrill that results when all the right ingredients—that elusive, perfect mix of brains, brawn, experience, and drive—somehow come together to produce a winner. Coming up with that mix and motivating the players who contribute to it is what separated my father from all but a few of his fellow head coaches. He knew that a successful team accepts one another's strengths, weaknesses, and unique contributions. He also knew that how members of the team interact with one another is one of the key determinants of success.

> *Business is a very complex machine, all of whose*
> *components are people, and as in a football team,*
> *it is vital that people mesh and gear smoothly.*

Mutual accountability: On Tuesdays, the Packers watched films of the previous Sunday's game. Each play was reviewed over and over as each player's effort was scrutinized and critiqued by Coach Lombardi in front of the entire team. In addition, by Thursday, the coaching staff had graded each player on every play, and the marks were posted in the locker room in plain sight for everyone to see.

The players feared Lombardi's midweek criticism, which motivated them to play well on Sunday. When Lombardi chewed you out on Tuesday, that was all the motivation you needed not to repeat that mistake again. After all, the last thing anyone on the team wanted was to let down his teammates. But each player's real concern and chief motivation was how their play on Sunday was going to appear to their teammates on Tuesday and Thursday. No one wanted his teammates to think he couldn't get the job done or that he didn't belong any longer.

Build for your team a feeling of oneness, of
dependence upon one another, and of strength to
be derived from unity.

TEAM IN ACTION: "THE LOMBARDI SWEEP"

The Lombardi principles were laid on the line every Sunday when the Packers took the field. Everything my father aspired to, from character in action to mental toughness, was put to the test on every snap of the football. That's when the results of all of his preparation and leadership became evident. (See Chapter 9 for more on results.) One play, perhaps above all others, best illustrates how common goals, complementary skills, and accountability came together to play a vital role in the Packers' success. Although the play did not originate in Green Bay, my father's Packers made it famous, so it seems right that the play became known as the "Packer Sweep," also referred to as the "Lombardi Sweep."

It might just have accurately been called the Giant Sweep, or maybe even the Ram Sweep. As a new assistant coach with the Giants, my father spent a lot of time early in 1954 studying films of a certain play run by the Rams. The Sweep was a running play that called for the guards and the fullback to lead the halfback around the end. After adding a few variations of his own, my father introduced it to the Giants that summer and made it a prominent part of his offensive game plan.

When it came to the Sweep, my father was relentless. He drilled that play into the soul of every player on the offense. He went over it again and again, chalk in hand, reviewing every assignment. He would sell and resell the goal of the play. "This is the lead play in our offense," he'd say, "We must make it go. We will make it go. We will run it again and again and again, and we will make it go."

"The one [play] everybody remembers most," coach and commentator John Madden later recalled, "is what came to be known as the Lombardi Sweep. Paul Hornung takes a handoff from Bart Starr and runs to his right behind the block of Jim Taylor, the fullback, and Jerry Kramer and Fuzzy Thurston, the two guards who had pulled out of the line."

The success of the Packer offense depended on the success of this one play. If everyone performed as the play was designed, the team succeeded, but if just one assignment was missed, the play would fail. The Packers would run the Sweep over and over, challenging their opponents to stop them. Inevitably, in adjusting to the Sweep, the opposing defense would leave themselves vulnerable to other plays in the Packer playbook. If you couldn't stop the Sweep, you couldn't beat the Packers. Quarterback Bart Starr watched my father get up at the blackboard and diagram this sequence of assignments—11 assignments, one for each player on the offense—every summer for nine straight years. He said that it was a brilliant performance, which captivated him every time he saw it.

> *There's nothing spectacular about it. It's just a yard-gainer, and I've diagrammed it so many times and coached it so much and watched it evolve so often since I first put it in with the Giants eight years ago that I think I see it in my sleep.*

I think my father was downplaying two important details when he made that statement. The first was his pride in the play. When the Sweep worked, it was a marvel to behold: 11 men with complementary skills, striving together, aiming for that all-important first down or touchdown.

The second was its grinding, relentless effectiveness. I once had a discussion with a player, a defensive tackle for the Dallas Cowboys, when both the Packers and the Cowboys were at the top of their game. He told me that in the week preceding a Packer–Cowboy game, the Cowboy defense would work almost exclusively on stopping the Sweep. He said that even though they practiced against the play all week—and often knew when the play was going to be run and how the Packers would run it—they *still* couldn't stop it.

Green Bay's opponents knew the play was coming, knew beyond certainty that those guards would be bearing down on them. Still, the Packers ran that play with an awesome efficiency, making the Sweep their hallmark. Lombardi felt that the Sweep helped to define the character of the team.

> *Behind all that is the basic truth that it*
> *expresses you as a coach and the players as a team,*
> *and they feel good when they execute it*
> *and it's completely right.*

Lombardi would have his offense practice this play over and over, stopping only when he was satisfied with the execution. The players would talk to themselves and each other (careful not to be overheard by the coach), and inevitably it would be a player who would yell "run it again" when they knew a mistake had been made. The Sweep helped pull the team together, as the players began to *hold each other accountable*, knowing in their hearts and minds that the endless repetition and grueling work was making them one, a team working together to win.

During those Tuesday film sessions and during every practice and meeting, Coach Lombardi drummed home the same message: Success means winning (*common goal*). And winning depends on the team's ability to execute, taking advantage of the strengths and accounting for the weaknesses of every player (*complementary skills*). And sound execution requires every player to do his part by carrying out his assignment (*mutual accountability*), confident in the knowledge that his teammates would be doing the same.

TWO LOMBARDI INGREDIENTS: SIMPLICITY AND FLEXIBILITY

I used the Packer Sweep as an illustration of how my father went about putting in place the fundamentals of team spirit: common goals, complementary skills and abilities, and mutual accountability. But I also used it to illustrate another key point about my father's approach to building a winning organization: *keeping it simple.*

In recent years, many authors and practitioners of management have embraced the idea captured in the acronym "KISS": *Keep it simple, stupid!* Vince Lombardi was an early subscriber to this formula. His playbook was simpler and smaller than most coaches. And his practices were often shorter, too. He didn't ask his players to commit dozens of complicated plays to memory. Instead, he asked his players to understand a small number of plays thoroughly and intimately, to make this small number of plays almost instinctual.

Once these few basic plays became second nature, he asked his players to become equally familiar with a dozen or more *options* that might be run off each of those core plays. Suddenly, the playbook included "hundreds" of plays, but they were organized logically and simply in each player's mind as collections of related options, simple, but full of possibilities.

Flexibility, intersected by discipline, was the key. The acclaimed book that my father wrote in 1963 with W. C. Heinz, *Run to*

Daylight, took its title from a technique employed by the Packer running backs to make the Sweep and other plays work. Simply put, most running plays involved the back running toward a designated spot in the line, hoping that the offensive linemen would open a hole to run through. While the Packer running backs did run the play that way, with the ballcarrier following his blockers, they were also trained to look for an *unexpected* opening, one that would allow the back to run to *daylight*.

Doing this is more difficult than it sounds. Timing is everything. To make running to daylight productive, several players, in an almost choreographed fashion, had to move in the same direction, responding quickly to the flow of the play. The blocker in front of the running back takes the defender in the direction the defender wants to go, and the back plays off of that—*bang, bang*—in a fraction of a second. For it to work, you have to have seen it, understood it, and run it about a thousand times. Discipline allows for creativity, which in turn allows for success.

LOMBARDI RULE #11

Innovate without complicating.

This isn't a universal prescription: An organization at death's door may have to innovate every which way (and may still go through the door). But innovations must reflect people's limited capacities to learn and to change. Be fair and realistic.

For all of these reasons, and more, my father was loath to depart from his game plan. Still, he would tip his hat to the inevitability of change, especially over the long term.

One must not hesitate to innovate and change with the times and the varying formations. The leader who stands still is not progressing, and he will not remain a leader for long.

But fundamentally, Lombardi believed in playing to one's strengths.

> *What it will all come down to again on Sunday,*
> *I'm thinking, is that we will both try to do what we*
> *do best. We know everything they can do, and*
> *they know everything we can do, so we will both*
> *go with our strength.*

Surprises, when appropriate, should come at the margins of your game and should be driven by inventiveness and speed. Surprises shouldn't be departures from the playbook, but refinements upon it.

> *The element of surprise may have temporary*
> *value . . . but both of us can be reasonably sure*
> *that the other team is not really going to change*
> *because only a grossly inferior team should ever*
> *depart or deviate from its strength to win. Even*
> *surprise should be based on deception and rapidity*
> *of maneuver, and not radical change.*

LOYALTY: CRITICAL AND ELUSIVE

Football teams depend on the development of an extraordinary cohesiveness, a unique bond, among a group of men who may have very little in common *except* for football. And at the same time, all members of the organization know that they are expendable. They may be here this year, performing brilliantly, but they may be gone next year, forging bonds with a whole new set of teammates.

Redskin cornerback Pat Fischer, reflecting on his time with Lombardi in 1969, commented on this paradox: "If you can be traded to help the team, then bam, you're gone. Yet, you're supposed to have loyalty toward the team and the coach, and you ask me, where is the loyalty that's supposed to be flowing back to me? . . . He's talking about very lofty, noble things, but how do you instill them when the underlying concern is insecurity?"

> ### *A professional football team is a kind of community of displaced persons.*

My father was well aware of this paradox, and there were definitely times when it troubled him. But he understood it to be one of the costs of doing business. He honestly loved the members of his team like family members and encouraged them to love each other; at the same time, he didn't hesitate to trade them away when he saw a way to improve the team. This was a *business*, after all. Lombardi knew that he, too, would be unceremoniously dumped if he ever came to be perceived as a liability to the team. It's not hard to call to mind coaches on both the college and professional levels, in football and other sports, who have fallen from grace with amazing speed and finality—heroes one year, scapegoats the next.

Today, of course, the relationship between a professional football player and his team is reversed by 180 degrees. Today's players have relative freedom of movement, and it is *their* loyalty, not their employer's, that is most often called into question. Logically, then, today's coach ought to be working doubly hard to instill loyalty and camaraderie in his players.

This is particularly true in a knowledge-based economy in which talent is at such a premium. Even more than my father and his business counterparts 30 years ago, leaders must seek out ways to woo and win the "volunteers" who make up today's workforce.

Accomplishing this is not as difficult a task as it sounds. (Review the lessons in the second half of this chapter for some good fundamentals.) Despite the mobility created by a strong economy, and despite the increasing "portability" of skills in a knowledge-based society, human nature really hasn't changed all that much. Just like the Green Bay Packers of the 1960s, people today want to be affiliated with a winning organization. They want to *award* their loyalty—and the effective leader finds ways to earn that award.

THE LOMBARDI RULES

Building the winning organization

Pick the right organization.
This isn't quite as obvious as it sounds. Where can you go where there's a lot of unrealized potential and where there's a rising tide?

Demand autonomy.
What do you absolutely have to control to make your job possible? If you can't get that degree of autonomy, you can't succeed.

Respect authority.
If you're going to ask people to respect your authority, you'll need to lead by example. Whatever hierarchy you're in—assuming its authority is legitimate—deserves your respect.

Delegate the second-tier stuff.
Look for existing competence in the organization, and take full advantage of that competence.

Check your hat.
Is your own position evolving? If so, how should the changes be reflected in your job description and those of others around you? Again, your successes should let you give things up.

Be brilliant, but don't be stubborn about it.
Yes, your job is to bring new insights and turn things around. But forcing a square peg into a round hole doesn't get either job done.

Import.
If there's someone out there who already knows your system and can help you survive the building or rebuilding period, grab him or her.

Build skills.
This is an important point in an era when people are demanding that organizations provide them with portable skills. You can't put big demands on people before you define and provide the needed skills.

Let 'em see you sweat.
Why should they kill themselves for the organization if you don't?

Build team spirit.

This means common goals, complementary skills and abilities, and mutual accountability.

Innovate without complicating.

This isn't a universal prescription: An organization at death's door may have to innovate every which way (and may still go through the door). But innovations must reflect people's limited capacities to learn and to change. Be fair and realistic.

Chapter 8

Motivating the Team to Extraordinary Performance

Conquests are won primarily in the hearts of men and once you have won their hearts, they'll follow you anywhere. Men will respond to this type of leadership in a most remarkable way. Success is based upon a spiritual quality, a power to inspire others.

Almost any vision, if it is sound, will succeed—as long as people are motivated and inspired to make it work. Leaders motivate and inspire people in many of the ways we've already discussed in Chapters 4 through 7. For example, they

- Display respect for others
- Show compassion
- Demonstrate courage and competence
- Exhibit and kindle passion
- Make sacrifices
- Have and demonstrate total commitment
- Work hard and demonstrate discipline
- Lead with integrity and build trust
- Shape and share a vision
- Identify and live their values
- Insist on excellence
- Inspire confidence

If you take the word "motivation" and add a letter here and there, you get "motive to act." "Motivation", then, can be defined as either a motive—an *inner* drive—or an *externally* imposed stimulus or incentive to act. "Inspiration" also implies a stimulus toward action, but adds a creative component. The power of the vision itself is a motivator. In Chapter 6, we talked about mission, vision, and values as ways to motivate people and move the organization forward. In this chapter, we will look more closely at some of the ways that my father motivated people.

If there was one thing that my father understood above all else, it was how to motivate and inspire people. My father felt that success depended on a leader's ability to get others to act. He was an expert in dealing with people, the best motivator in his business and—in my own experience—better than most in other businesses, too. In this chapter, I draw out the key lessons on how to motivate both *teams* and *individuals*, and I discuss ways to apply these lessons to the workplace.

Leaders motivate and inspire by creating a climate for success. They motivate by kindling passion, painting a picture of success (through mission, vision, and values), fanning the flame of team spirit, and inspiring confidence. They motivate by demanding accountability, and obtaining results. These themes recur throughout this book, but they have special significance when seen through the lens of motivation.

> *Success is based upon a spiritual quality,*
> *a power to inspire others.*

SETTING THE MOTIVATIONAL TABLE

Today, perhaps more than ever before, people are examining *what* they're doing and *why* they're doing it. This is not a cosmetic change or a small shifting of priorities. Rather, it's a real sea change in the way people look at their lives.

One reason this has happened is that employers have broken almost all the rules that used to govern the employer–employee relationship. We've all seen the list of offenses a thousand times: downsizing, reorganizing, re-engineering, inept or insensitive intrusions of technology, excessive executive compensation, managers interested only in short-term results, and managers who micromanage rather than lead.

Collectively, these processes and patterns assault us and drain us of our spirit. We become frightened and insecure. Our morale and job satisfaction plummet. The most competent people are unwilling to work under such trying conditions and leave for greener pastures. People with fewer options try to hang on. Then, instead of growing more skilled and flexible, the organization becomes less skilled and more hidebound. There is a reason the cartoon character "Dilbert" strikes a chord with so many people.

In study after study on the subject of motivation, researchers have demonstrated that the key motivator is not necessarily money, security, or status. Instead, most people are motivated by the desire to feel important and to make a difference. If you doubt this, then why is it that people in jobs that pay well and give employees recognition and a challenge are unmotivated? And why do we see motivated people in jobs that provide few of these external motivators?

People are motivated by things that promise to give their lives purpose and meaning. And since they spend so many of their waking hours at work, they naturally look to the workplace to provide this kind of meaning. Small wonder, then, that a bad employer feels, in a sense, like a betrayal!

We hunger for a self that we can be proud of. Like Thoreau, we don't want to discover, at the moment of our death, that we have failed to live. We want work we can get excited about. We want work we can tell our family and friends about, with honest delight.

Your job as a leader is to give people what they want. Remember, even if they tell you otherwise, they want far more than a paycheck. They also want *meaning*. If they don't get it from you, they'll go looking for some other place to find it. Failing to engage yourself and your people in meaningful, purposeful work is to ignore the highest, truest motivation: "meaning."

LOMBARDI RULE #1

Offer people meaning.
If you don't, someone else will.

"Meaning," of course, comes from within. In Chapter 3, I wrote about self-discovery as the path to self-knowledge, which in turn is the foundation for meaning and purpose. In recent years, many companies, well aware of the litany of complaints and offenses cited a few paragraphs ago, have tried to create cultures that encourage self-discovery. They have challenged members of their organizational team to state what's really important and suggest ways to move the organization in that direction.

If you are in a position to set policy in this direction, I suggest you do so with all due speed. Let the people who work for you tell you what's important to them. You may not agree with their conclusions; or you may want to go way beyond what they tell you; but at least you'll have a strong point of departure as you try to set the motivational table.

My father, head of a relatively small organization in a simpler era, mostly played it by ear when he set out to motivate his players. But I think his style reflects an intuitive awareness about the relative importance of *money* and *meaning* in the workplace. In fact, he went out of his way (as general manager) to keep the lid on the payroll; but he went just as far out of his way (as coach) to give meaning to people's lives.

He sought to motivate people on two levels: the team level and the individual level. I'll look at these two levels separately, although the division is a little artificial. My father was always doing both things and would have been hard pressed to tell you whether a particular tactic was aimed at just one person or at many people. Many times he did things that seemed to be aimed at an individual, but were just as much aimed at reaching the entire team.

KEEP THE PRESSURE ON

Deep down, Lombardi understood that leaders don't truly motivate. Lou Holtz, the successful Notre Dame coach who now coaches at the University of South Carolina, expressed his grasp of this simple truth when he said, "Motivation is simple: You eliminate those who aren't motivated." *People motivate themselves.*

Your task as a leader is to *inspire* your people with a "motive to act," an incentive to adapt, if they haven't found one for themselves. You inspire your people with the vision that they want to see brought to a successful conclusion.

Yet paradoxically, you also get people moving by painting a compelling picture of the consequences of *not* adapting to change. You do this by showing what happened to companies that failed to adapt and by asking, "Is this what we want to happen to us?" You do this by subjecting people to enough stress and pressure that they realize that they must either adapt or fail. You create enough pressure to unfreeze the culture and the entrenched hierarchy— enough stress to force people out of their comfort zone and the mind-set of "This is the way we've always done it here."

All I want to know is how far I can push a guy.

My father understood that a leader must perform a balancing act: pacing the rate of adaptation, keeping the pressure on to get people to move, and, at the same time, making the workplace safe enough to maintain an adaptive learning environment.

LOMBARDI RULE #2

> **Keep enormous pressure on.**
> But stay within the individual and organizational breaking points.

Again, this is one of the keys to Lombardi's leadership success. Lombardi put enormous pressure on his players. He pushed, and he pushed, and then he pushed some more. In so many words, he was asking his players a pointed question: If they couldn't handle the pressure he was putting on them in practice, how would they be able to stand up to the pressure of a championship game, on national television, perhaps in front of 70,000 hostile fans?

Not every leader can do it the way Lombardi did it, nor should they. But somehow, you as a leader, must determine how your people will perform in a pressure situation. Will they make mistakes? Will they fold and quit on you, at least figuratively? The questions are real ones, because sooner or later, you will be in your version of a championship game. Then, it will be too late to compensate if your people don't come through for you.

> *The most important thing a coach needs is the knowledge that his team can or can't play under pressure. If it can't, you need new players; if it can, you can make do with average.*

Lombardi's Packers could handle pressure. For nine years, he applied more and more pressure. Big games, to them, were just more of the same. Lombardi's championship teams of 1961 and 1962 had as much talent as, or more talent than, any other team they played. The '65, '66, and '67 championship teams, however, were not on a par, talentwise, with some of their opponents. So how did they continue to win championships? They handled the pressure of the big game better than their opponents. *They never beat themselves.*

Two pivotal games illustrate this point, both played against the Dallas Cowboys, both played to determine who would represent the NFL in the first two Super Bowls. The first was in 1966, played in Dallas. The Cowboys had the ball in the closing minutes. They made a critical mistake, failed to score, and, as a result, went on to lose the game to the Packers. The following year, in Green Bay, it was the Packers who had the ball in the closing minutes. They played mistake-free football and scored, thereby winning the critical game.

My father started with the assumption that professional football teams were more or less at parity—that the money, the players, and the coaching were more or less comparable. What distinguished a winning team from a losing team was often its level of inspiration and motivation. It was a taxing, draining, "maddening" (his word), burdensome, and sometimes boring job.

> *This is not easy, this effort, day after day, week*
> *after week, to keep them up, but it is essential.*
> *Each week there is a different challenge, but there*
> *is also that unavoidable degree of sameness to*
> *these meetings.*

And to some extent, the rougher parts of the job didn't come naturally to him. Remember that he had once considered becoming a priest and, later, a teacher. The rough-and-tumble of pro football, the emotion, the yelling, releasing players who have played their hearts out for you, just the *hardness* of the coaching profession, sometimes weighed heavily on him.

> *It's no damn fun being hard. I've been doing this*
> *for years and years and years. It's never been great*
> *fun. You have to drive yourself constantly.*
> *I don't enjoy it. It takes a hell of a lot out of me.*
> *And, Christ, you get kind of embarrassed with*
> *yourself sometimes. You berate somebody,*
> *and you feel disgusted with yourself for doing it,*
> *for being in a job where you have to.*
> *Fortunately, I don't remember.*

But this was his *job*—the job of a motivational and inspirational leader. So he kept the pressure on his team, and he kept the pressure on himself.

MOTIVATING THE TEAM: THE POWER OF *FIRE* AND *PRAISE*

Coach Lombardi had a challenging task: to find a way to motivate and inspire several dozen prima donnas, many of whom had spent much of their childhood and adolescence as local heroes, with their physical accomplishments celebrated and their shortcomings mostly ignored.

> *I am going to find 36 men who have the pride to make any sacrifice to win. There are such men. If they're not here, I'll get them. If you are not one, if you don't want to play, you might as well leave right now.*

That's what my father told the Green Bay Packers on July 23, 1959, the day he first met with them officially as head coach. In making this speech, Vince Lombardi was taking a calculated risk. It was extremely difficult to get a handle on this group of men. They were enormously frustrated following their miserable 1–10–1 record the previous year. Even so, it was no sure bet that they would buy into this new guy, either. Who was he, after all? Only an assistant coach from New York. My father half expected a number of these players—some of the veterans, at least—to take him up on his offer to "leave right now."

As it turned out, no one left. The gamble paid off: Lombardi had reached into them, found their pride as professionals, and put that pride on the table. *If you don't have pride*, he said, *leave now.* No one left.

> *When two teams meet that are equal in ability and execution, it's the team that has pride that wins.*

My father used every trick in the book to get his teams up for a game. "Trick" isn't exactly the right word, because it implies deception. Lombardi didn't deceive his players in order to motivate them; they would have seen through him immediately. But he wasn't above a little play-acting either. I remember one day I saw him before practice. He was in a pretty good mood. I don't recall the specifics, but I remember thinking that he wasn't the holy terror that the team might have been expecting. A few minutes later, I happened to pass by the open door of his locker room. I looked in and saw him standing in front of the mirror, practicing a range of menacing and hostile facial expressions. He was putting on his "game face."

> ### I'm just going to give these guys complete hell today. . . . Today is going to be one of those days.

"Giving the team hell" was certainly a big piece of my father's motivational/inspirational approach. On Tuesdays, the players would watch the game film from the previous Sunday. Players who had performed poorly knew that they were in for a semi-public humiliation. It could get *hot* in that locker room—and it usually did.

At the first film session after a critical loss to the Rams in 1965, for example, Lombardi ripped into the team with all the force that his leathery lungs and raspy voice could command. "You guys don't care if you win or lose," he yelled. "I'm the only one that cares. I'm the only one that puts his blood and guts and his heart into the game! You guys show up, you listen a little bit, you concentrate …you've got the concentration of three-year-olds! You're nothing! I'm the only guy that gives a damn if we win or lose!"

This display provoked a near mutiny. Forrest Gregg, a perennial All-Pro offensive tackle, jumped to his feet in a threatening pose, looking as if he intended to plow his way up to the front of the room and take my father on. As several of his teammates restrained him, Gregg shouted in no uncertain terms that he deeply resented my father's comments. Another player, Bob Skoronski, jumped up and said more or less the same thing. How *dare* you imply that we don't care, that we don't want to win? Tension filled the room. Had

Lombardi gone too far? Had he stepped over an invisible line and lost the respect of his players? Had his motivational technique—if it was a technique, as opposed to a pure display of temper—backfired?

LOMBARDI RULE #3

Motivate the group.
Find ways to move people *en masse.*

"All right," barked my father enthusiastically, switching gears with astonishing ease. "Now that's the kind of attitude I want to see! Who else feels that way?" The answer, of course, was that everybody felt that way. First one person got up, then another, and then another. Eventually, my father had the whole team on its feet, expressing its desire and determination to win.

Other times, particularly after a good (but losing) effort, my father would take an entirely different approach.

Perhaps you didn't realize you could have won this game. But I think there's no doubt in your minds now. And that's why you will win it all next year. This will never happen again. You will never lose another championship.

That's what he told the team after Green Bay lost the championship game to Philadelphia in 1960. Some people have misread this kind of "inconsistency" as pure manipulation, an effort to keep everybody guessing, off balance, on edge, on their toes. What's Coach going to do next? There *was* some of that at play here. But mainly, I think that in both cases, he was expressing his emotions honestly. I think he was also using the specifics of the two defeats—one sloppy and filled with mistakes, the other courageous—to steer the team toward a better outcome next time. It was just a matter of different situations, different tactics.

There is a time when violent reactions are in order.
And there are times when purring like a pussycat
and bestowing thanks and gratitude are equally
desirable. Each of us must learn when the time fits
the response, and must tailor our action or
reaction to each situation.

Sometimes my father would work the team into a near-frenzy before a critical game. Bill Forrester, a linebacker on Lombardi's early Packer teams, says he sustained his worst injury of Lombardi's first season in Green Bay when he jumped up and smashed his elbow against his locker after listening to my father's pep talk before a game against the Bears. Another player once begged my father to "Stop, stop!" in the middle of his pre-game pep talk. It was *too much, too much.*

But he was just as capable of pushing the team in the other direction. As he boarded the bus that would take the Packers to the first-ever "superbowl" game against the Kansas City Chiefs, Lombardi stepped into the middle of the aisle and got the team's attention. Then, to everyone's amazement, he did a soft-shoe dance in the aisle and sat down. "What was that all about," an astounded assistant asked him. "They were too tight," my father responded matter-of-factly.

LOMBARDI RULE # 4

Counter expectations.
Sometimes, the least expected motivational device is the best.

Before a game against the arch-rival Bears in 1967, he skipped the high-volume exhortation that many of the Packers must have been expecting. Instead, he told a joke, keying off the fact that the area around Green Bay had been settled many years earlier by Belgian immigrants. "Did you ever hear why Belgians are so strong?"

"No, Coach," came the reply. "Why?"

"Because they raise dumbbells."

The Packers groaned at this lame attempt at humor. (It was, in fact, a joke the Belgian-Americans told on themselves, and many in the room had heard it before.) They razzed their unpredictable coach and took the field. "It took the edge off the tension," Jerry Kramer later commented, demonstrating very well that he understood his coach's motivational techniques.

Vince Lombardi placed a great deal of emphasis on team bonding as a way to motivate his players. He cultivated a number of rituals—mandatory singing by first-year men during training camp, buffet dinners after preseason games with friends and family invited, Thanksgiving dinner with the entire team and their families, all the players wearing green sport coats with the Packer logo on the breast pocket when they traveled as a team—all done to motivate the players and get them to think as a unit. Not offense or defense, rookie or veteran, black or white, but a *team*.

This technique dated back at least to his days with the Giants, many of whom lived near each other and socialized together. Lombardi was quite successful at re-creating this culture in Green Bay, with its small-town atmosphere. With only one year in Washington, he didn't have the time to pull it off a third time. Certainly, the challenge would have been greater, since the Redskins were scattered across the Washington metropolitan area.

INSPIRING THE INDIVIDUAL:
TREAT DIFFERENT PLAYERS *DIFFERENTLY*

Great teams are groups of talented individuals who subordinate their personal styles and goals to those of the team. But even the most disciplined teams—I'm thinking of the Packers under my father and the Boston Celtics under the legendary Red Auerbach— are still a collection of individuals, who need to be treated as individuals. Again, my father was a master of this critical leadership art.

One of Lombardi's players, defensive tackle Henry Jordan, once made a celebrated comment: "Lombardi treats us all alike. Like dogs!" But in fact, the opposite was true: My father carefully distinguished among his players, feeding individual egos without pitting one teammate against another. One technique he used was a formal "grading system." Grades for individual performances on Sunday were posted on Thursdays, and in a mock-serious team ceremony, Lombardi handed out $5 bills (and later, $10 bills) to the highest performing individuals. The Green Bay Packers weren't overpaid, but they certainly didn't need the money.

What they did need, and what everyone needs, was the chance to be recognized by their coach and their peers for outstanding individual performances. Part of the art of motivating individuals lies in doing your homework. My father (whom Green Bay star Max McGee once referred to as "the greatest psychologist") tried to learn everything possible about the emotional makeup of his individual players and then use that knowledge to its best effect. "The truth is," halfback Donny Anderson once told a reporter, "he was a psychologist more than a slave driver. He had a mental master plan for getting the best out of everybody." This meant treating different players differently.

> *You can't coach without criticizing, and it's essential to understand how to criticize each man individually. For instance, some can take constructive criticism in front of a group, and some can't. Some can take it privately, but others can only take it indirectly. Football is a pressure business, and on my teams I put on most of the pressure. The point is that I've got to learn 40 ways to pressure 40 men.*

In other words, my father had a mental inventory of all of his players and a clear sense of how to "pressure" (or motivate) each of them. For example, Henry Jordan had a problem with complacency.

*[Jordan] has a tendency to be satisfied, which
is why I don't flatter him much, and why often,
when we're reviewing the pictures, I make him a
target. Sometimes you will make a man a target to
impress somebody else who can't accept public
criticism, but I will call Hank because we both
know his ability and know that I'm on him to
bring it out, and because he performs best when
he's just a little upset.*

Another interesting example was quarterback Bart Starr, who couldn't perform under my father's standard tactic of semi-public humiliation, whether on the field or in the locker room. One day, after being yelled at by my father for throwing an interception during practice, Starr asked for a closed-door meeting with Lombardi. The young quarterback bravely made the point that if he was expected to lead the team on the field, he couldn't afford to be undercut by Lombardi's sometimes harsh criticisms in front of the team. Lombardi agreed with this reasoning—(no doubt also taking the measure of this quiet young man from a military family) and agreed not to criticize him in front of his teammates again. Lombardi kept his end of the bargain, and from that day forward, the Lombardi–Starr combination was enormously effective.

My father's handling of his next star quarterback, Sonny Jurgensen of the Redskins, was equally revealing of his motivational/inspirational techniques. Jurgensen, a supremely talented athlete, had a reputation as a playboy who knew how to enjoy himself off the field. (Some of his teammates later said that the legend far outstripped the fact, but Jurgensen himself enjoyed fueling the legend.) I think it's safe to assume that Jurgensen was anxious about his first meeting with his new coach: The legendary rounder Jurgensen meets the equally legendary disciplinarian Lombardi!

"I walked into his office in Washington not knowing what to expect," Jurgensen later recalled. "After we shook hands, he looked at me and said, 'Sonny, I want you to be yourself. Just be what you are.' What a thing to say! Jeez, right then I felt like running into a wall, anything to let him know I would do whatever he wanted of me."

"It's the motivation that's the thing," commented Hall of Fame fullback Jim Taylor a few years after my father's death, "and he knew just the right words, just the right approach to me. He knew how to handle me just like a parent handles his children to get the maximum out of them. Just the right approach to get me to listen, that was it. And he motivated me to the maximum. I don't think I could have given more."

LOMBARDI RULE #5

Motivate the individual.
Nothing, after all, is more personal.

Max McGee, one of my fathers' favorite players, tells a story that is a good example of how each player was treated fairly, yet differently. During preseason camp, the Packers ran a drill known as the "nutcracker." This was my father's favorite drill; the players, on the other hand, hated it.

It went like this: Two tackling dummies were laid parallel to each other a few feet apart. Two players—an offensive player and a defensive player—would line up nose to nose inside the dummies. An offensive back would line up behind the offensive player. At the snap of the ball, the offensive player would try to drive the defensive player backwards, giving the running back room enough to run by while staying inside the dummies. The collisions that took place during this drill practically shook the ground. It was a drill that taught the fundamentals of blocking and tackling, but it was also a test of your manhood, played out in front of the entire team.

McGee, a wide receiver, wanted no part of this action. As a wide receiver, he wouldn't be asked to make this kind of a block, and in the past he had suffered a number of head injuries. So McGee went to Lombardi and explained the situation to him. My father told McGee that he couldn't excuse him from the drill. On the other hand, if McGee could find a way to stay out of the "nutcracker," my father wouldn't go out of his way to say anything about it.

And that's what happened. For nine years, McGee never took part in the "nutcracker." Curiously, over those nine years, McGee's teammates never realized that he was escaping participation in the much-dreaded drill.

This is a case where Lombardi showed flexibility in a special situation. Ultimately, however, leadership comes down to doing the difficult things. You have to push and pull your people beyond their own perceived limits. You have to continually test your people. What motivates and inspires them? How much pressure can you apply, and how will they respond? Will they align with the vision? You will be called upon to do things that are unpopular. If you want to be popular and well liked, you won't push as hard, because you don't want people to dislike you. The desire to be liked interferes with the hard decisions a leader must make.

> ### *I hold it more important to have the players' confidence than their affection.*

Lombardi had disagreements with a number of the people who reported to him, as all leaders do. And like most leaders, Lombardi had a few people who rebelled against his way of leadership. They went somewhere else, and he stayed. The interesting thing is that almost every one of his players, even the ones who left, still respected him.

L O M B A R D I   R U L E   # 6

Win respect; affection may follow.
Respect motivates. Win their respect first.

"When I think of him," Redskins' offensive guard Ray Schoenke once said, "I don't think of warmth. I don't think of sensitivity. If he was sensitive, he certainly wouldn't have said some of the things he said to me. . . . As much as I hated the guy, and I did—I *hated* him!—I had tremendous respect for him. Tremendous. I played some of my best football of my life under him. . . . It is a paradox."

Paradox is a concept that was introduced early in this book. It is critical in understanding leadership. And it's a word that comes up often when you speak to the people who worked with and for my father. With calculation, he found ways to get you to do things you didn't know you were capable of doing.

> *There are some people I knew I couldn't push.*
> *Some people I had my doubts about, and I pushed*
> *them and berated them to find out what I could*
> *about their character, their limits. Those are the*
> *things that are important to me, because this is*
> *what the game is all about.*

I shouldn't give the reader the impression that Vince Lombardi was always acting according to a logical plan when he was motivating his players. Nothing could be further from the truth. He was at times a spontaneously warm, genuine, and compassionate individual who privately took steps to help his players through troubled times. When a player's son broke his leg, Lombardi called the hospital to check on the boy's progress. When a player's mother died in an auto accident, Lombardi arranged to fly that player home and have a wreath of flowers sent. There were countless incidents like these, most of which went unnoticed by anyone except those directly involved. He laughed and cried openly with his players. He lived their lives with them, and that, for many, was enormously motivating.

And of course, there was another side of Vince Lombardi's spontaneity and emotionality. With the exception of Starr and a few others like him who couldn't perform at their best when yelled at, my father would get *passionately, furiously,* mad at people. He would let them know about their mistakes on the spot, in real time. He would break an individual down to rock bottom, with an emotional tongue-lashing that could be absolutely devastating. I witnessed many of these verbal assaults, and I was often deeply embarrassed when it happened. These players were my heroes. And it must be said that I was on the receiving end of many of these verbal dressing-downs. We had a lot in common, those players and I.

> *Hell, I can't just sit around and see an error being made and not say anything about it. I like to think I've had some experience in this business, and you don't win when you're making a lot of errors. Nobody wants to be told they're making errors, not the way I tell them. But they've got to be told until they get to the point where they don't make them anymore.*

And then, an hour later or a day later, he'd be patting that same player on the back, telling him that things were going well and that there were no hard feelings. In many of those cases, I think he realized he had gone too far, and now it was time to rebuild some bridges. "If I yell at someone," he used to say, "five minutes later I don't know what I said or who I said it to." And that was true, as far as it went, although there were many times at home when I could only wish he was that quick to forget!

Other times, I think, the Lombardi roller-coaster ride was far more deliberate. He was determined to get "the last 10 percent" out of people, and sometimes an emotional explosion was the best way to accomplish that. This approach flies in the face of most modern motivational theory, which argues that criticism should be *private* and applause should be *public*. Many a Packer (and later a

Redskin) wished that my father could have been a more modern thinker. But I have to admit that it did work with a lot of people. Some people, it seemed, clearly benefited from the tension–crisis–explosion–resolution cycle at which my father excelled.

MOTIVATING BY DEGREES

Motivation is not a one-step fix. It's not one game; it's a 16-game season, plus the playoffs. It involves *reinforcement* and a process of *adaptation* to new ways of thinking. As a leader, you must break down this "season of adaptation" into manageable parts. You need to create momentum, through short-term wins that give credibility and staying power to your vision. People must periodically see that their efforts are producing results.

If, in the summer of 1959, Coach Lombardi had talked exclusively about a world championship to a 1–10–1 team, he would have lost them. He would have been too far out in front. Talking "championship" would have been de-motivating.

Lombardi understood that winning a championship was but the last in a series of victories. To win the NFL Championship, the Packers needed to win the Conference Championship. To win the Conference Championship they had to win their division. To win the division title, they needed to win more games than the other teams in their division.

> *Changes take time.*
> *They do not take place overnight.*

Over the course of a long season, victories come in all kinds of shapes and sizes. Victory in a particular game, for example, requires the execution of goals on offense, defense, and special teams. Goals are further broken down by position. Linemen have goals for the game, as do the receivers, the quarterback, the running backs, and the defense. Every player, moreover, has a goal for each play.

Coach Lombardi preached to his players that most games are won by only a few specific plays. Since no one knew which play was going to win the game, each player had to give 100 percent on every play.

Motivate by inches.
Better to begin with small victories than large frustrations.

The goal of winning the championship, therefore, had to be built on the foundation of a thousand small victories. It depended on each player seeing the connection between his individual effort and winning the championship. It depended on motivation and inspiration by degree: people being encouraged by each small victory to move on to the next challenge.

INVOLVE KEY PLAYERS

When my father joined the New York Giants as an assistant in 1954, he brought a reputation of being an outstanding high school and college coach, but he was new to professional football. He understood the running game, but was not well grounded in the passing attack as the pros played it. He might have taken the stance, "Hey, I'm the coach; you'll do it *my* way." Instead, he chose to ask some of the veteran players for help.

During his first training camp, after the evening meeting Lombardi would walk over to the players' dorm and kick around a play he had put in that afternoon. Could it be run better? Once veteran players like Frank Gifford, Charlie Conerly, and Kyle Rote understood that Lombardi was sincere in asking for their help, they opened up and shared their knowledge with him.

During film work with both the Giants and Packers, there was a surprising amount of interplay between the coaches and players.

Players like Hornung, Starr, and Gregg drew on their vast experience to suggest things that could work and also voiced their opinion as to what wouldn't work. Studying game film the week before the 1967 NFL Championship against the Dallas Cowboys, for example, Jerry Kramer—All-Pro guard for the Packers for many years, noticed that the player across from him, Cowboy defensive tackle Jethro Pugh, stood up at the snap of the ball. Kramer thought that in a short-yardage situation, he could get under Pugh and leverage him out of the way. He mentioned this to Lombardi, and a play was put in to take advantage of Kramer's observation.

Although he didn't know it at the time, Kramer's experienced read of Pugh would play a major role in the championship game. The Packers won the 1967 title on the last play of the game, with Bart Starr running a quarterback sneak behind Kramer's block on Pugh. Despite his reputation as a martinet, Vince Lombardi was a leader who listened to his people.

Years later, Kramer told me a story that happened the year my father retired as coach of the Packers. They were getting ready to play their arch-rivals, the Chicago Bears. The challenge was how to block Dick Butkus, the great Chicago middle linebacker. The coaching staff put in a blocking scheme that Kramer—who had played against Butkus for many years—*knew* wouldn't work. When Jerry pointed this out to the coaches, they wouldn't listen, and he was told to block the way it was drawn up. Jerry decided then and there to retire at the end of the season.

LOMBARDI RULE #8

Go where the wisdom is.
People want to help you and the organization succeed.
It *motivates* them.

When Lombardi put in a new play on offense, he would ask his veteran players, offensive and defensive, for their opinion as to whether the play could work. This accomplished two things. First, he got an expert opinion from people who had seen similar plays over the years. Second, he made those players feel that they were part of things—that the play was their idea and they had an investment in its success.

Motivation is fostered in an atmosphere of mutual respect. Good leaders are confident and comfortable enough with themselves that they freely accept opinions from others, including opinions that are diametrically opposed to their own. They know they don't have all the answers. They look for input, debate, and discussion before making a decision. They understand that they don't learn very much from people who agree with them all the time.

They understand that empowerment is not so much a process as it is an atmosphere of respect, created by a leader who listens more than he or she expounds. Leaders enjoy a diversity of opinions. They enjoy a good argument, based on contesting ideas. They're not afraid of having strong people around them. They will put up with a few "characters" if their offbeat contributions to team chemistry outweigh the distractions they may create.

> *The achievements of an organization are the*
> *results of the combined efforts of each individual.*

Sam Huff, the All-Pro linebacker who played for the New York Giants for many years and later was a player–coach under Lombardi with the Redskins, spoke to this point. "He wanted you to stand up to him, to fight back," Huff said. "When he'd get mad at someone, he'd go back to his office and say, 'I wish the SOB would stand up and say what he thinks.'"

LESSONS FOR TODAY

As pointed out in Chapter 7, my father exercised an extraordinary degree of power within the Packer organization. Also, as noted earlier, pro football players in the 1960s had no freedom of movement. Unlike today, players couldn't move from one team to another. Once a Packer, always a Packer, unless, of course, Lombardi decided to trade you or release you. So he was able to create his own approach to motivating people, and he was also able to get rid of the guys whom he couldn't find ways to motivate and inspire. Even people who didn't particularly care for my father and didn't like his management style found this possibility of being traded away a highly motivating factor.

The realities of the larger world also conspired to make motivation easier in my father's day. Back when he took over as head coach in Green Bay, almost no one in professional football was making big money. Only a superstar could command more than $50,000 a year. Players worked during the off-season—managing stores, selling insurance, running oil rigs—and didn't expect to play many seasons. Benefits were almost nonexistent, at least by today's standards.

So people played for my father mainly because they wanted to be a part of the *World Champion Green Bay Packers.* They took great pride in their success—success they would not be enjoying elsewhere. They knew that despite the yelling and the criticism, Green Bay was the best place to be for a pro football player.

Well, obviously, it's a lot tougher today. Nowadays, even in hierarchical contexts like the church, the military, and professional sports, people expect to participate in the design of their jobs. They expect to shape their own assignments and pick their own teammates, and in many cases they should. Especially in a booming economy, people consider themselves to be "volunteers" in their jobs, and volunteers don't expect to be yelled at and criticized in front of their fellow workers.

But maybe the seeming gulf between my father's motivational approach and the approach needed to lead a contemporary organization isn't so large after all. Vince Lombardi was about finding great people, getting organizational obstacles out of their way, using their talents to the best effect, and constantly pushing them to new heights, levels of accomplishment that they might not have dreamed of on their own. He was about putting all these motivating/inspiring factors together in one compelling, comprehensible package: himself.

The package wasn't always pretty. "He was tough and abusive and at times he was downright nasty," Bart Starr once commented publicly. But Starr was a perceptive player who understood the package. "The shoutings, encouragements, inspirational messages, and vindictive assault on mistakes transcended the walls of our dressing rooms," he once wrote in a letter to my father, "but in the privacy of those same rooms to have known the bigger man—kneeling in tearful prayer with his players, after both triumph and defeat—was a strengthening experience that only your squads can ever fully appreciate."

A "strengthening experience": Isn't that what inspirational, motivational leadership and great organizations are all about?

THE LOMBARDI RULES

Motivating the team to extraordinary performance

Offer people meaning.
If you don't, someone else will.

Keep enormous pressure on.
But stay within the individual and organizational breaking points.

Motivate the group.
Find ways to move people *en masse.*

Counter expectations.
Sometimes, the least expected motivational device is the best.

Motivate the individual.
Nothing, after all, is more personal.

Win respect; affection may follow.
Respect motivates. Win their respect first.

Motivate by inches.
Better to begin with small victories than large frustrations.

Go where the wisdom is.
People want to help you and the organization succeed.
It *motivates* them.

Chapter 9

Vince Lombardi on Winning

I'm here because we win.
You're here because we win.
When we lose we're gone.

Minutes before the kickoff for Super Bowl II, Coach Lombardi called his players together and made a short speech. This is what he said:

It's very difficult for me to say anything. Anything I say would be repetitious. This is our 23rd game this year. I don't know anything else I could tell this team. Boys, you are a good football team. You are a proud football team. You are the world champions of the National Football League, for the third time in a row, for the first time in the history of the National Football League. That's a great thing to be proud of.

But let me just say this: All the glory, everything you've had is going to be small in comparison to winning this one. This is a great thing for you. You're the only team in the history of the National Football League to ever have this opportunity to win the Super Bowl twice. Boys, I tell you I'd be so proud of that, I just fill myself up with myself. I just get bigger and bigger.

It's not going to come easy. This is a club that's gonna hit you. They're gonna try and hit you, and you've got to take it out of them. You've got to be 40 tigers out there. That's all. Just run. Just block and tackle. If you do that, there's no question what the answer's going to be in this ball game. Keep your poise. You've faced them all. There's nothing they can show you out there you haven't faced a hundred times before. Right?

This locker room speech, short as it is, embodies many of the leadership elements emphasized in this book. *Vision:* "You're the only team in the history of the NFL to ever have this opportunity to win the Super Bowl twice." *Pride:* "You are a proud football team." *Challenge:* "This is a club that's gonna hit you." *Discipline:* " Keep your poise." *Mental toughness:* "They're gonna try and hit you, and you've got to take it out of them." *Motivation/Inspiration:* "…everything you've done is going to be small compared to this." *Excellence:* "You are the World Champions." *Passion:* "You've got to be 40 tigers out there." *Confidence:* "There's nothing they can show you out there you haven't faced a hundred times." *Commitment:* "It's not going to come easy." *Results:* "If you do that, there's no question what the answer's going to be in this ball game."

This brings us to the final element of Lombardi's leadership model: *results*, the answer, the outcome, the ultimate effect. It all comes down to this all-important consequence of your leadership abilities. The absence of results renders your leadership meaningless. Bookstores are full of the debate about organizational structure: hierarchical or flat, centralized or decentralized, divisional or nondivisional, and everything in between. Yet it's not structure, but results, that truly make a leader. Leadership is not a position; it's a process that produces the desired results. If you don't produce results—if you can't execute—you are not a leader.

> *Some of us will do our jobs well and some of will not,*
> *but we will all be judged on one thing: the result.*

Leaders get paid for results, not for being right. Results come from mistakes—being wrong—and leaders must possess Lombardi's mental toughness to handle mistakes, take accountability for them, and quickly abandon those efforts that fail to produce results.

If you are right all the time, you are not taking enough risks. Results require a willingness to act, even if you are unsure of what lies ahead. Only through action and risk can you take your company to the next level.

> *Boldness: We make way for the man who boldly pushes past us. Who bravely dares must sometimes risk all.*

Results, specific and measurable, come from having a clear vision, defining what improvement and adaptation look like, and having a beginning and end in mind.

Results come from knowing what you are achieving today and having a clear, specific strategy for closing the gap between today's reality and your vision for tomorrow.

Perhaps you don't want to be a "Lombardi" type of leader, challenging, demanding, at times intimidating. Maybe you don't believe you can be that kind of leader. That's fine, as long as you can produce results with whatever style you prefer. But keep in mind that ultimately, it's not whether your people like you or approve of you; it's whether they *produce* for you.

> *The leader does not exist in the abstract, but rather in terms of what he does in a specific situation.*

People make a great deal of the rings that are awarded to the teams that win the Super Bowl. And because Vince Lombardi's teams won the first two of these contests—even before the words "super bowl" became one word and got capitalized—he had the privilege of inventing a few traditions. One of these was designing the rings worn by the winners of those championship games.

The ring that the Green Bay Packers wear for defeating the Oakland Raiders in Super Bowl II has three large diamonds across the face. The three diamonds signify the three consecutive world championships won by the Packers, with Super Bowl II being the third. When my father died, I inherited this ring, and I often wear it to speaking engagements and other public occasions.

On one side of the ring are the words "RUN TO WIN." The phrase is a biblical verse my father gave the players the week before the game. He quoted St. Paul:

> *Do you know that all who run in a race, all indeed run. But only one receives the prize. So run to win.*
>
> Corinthians 9:24

It seems to me that any discussion of results and of my father's approach to being number one would be incomplete without a broader treatment about what Vince Lombardi thought about winning—and losing—and making one's best effort. If people know anything about my father, they know he was a ferocious competitor. But if that's as far as their understanding goes, they're missing some very important things.

LOMBARDI RULE #1

> **Run to win.**
> Set a high standard for your team, and keep that standard out in front (on the wall, on your ring, in your mission statement) where all can see it.

There are few subjects on which my father made more comments than the subject of winning—in other words, results. And, as we'll see, a couple of those comments he wound up wishing he'd never made.

IS WINNING EVERYTHING?

Let's start with the most controversial comment of all:

Winning isn't everything; it's the only thing.

I'm constantly amazed at the number of people who know nothing about my father except that (1) he was a football coach and (2) he uttered (or endorsed or seemed to have endorsed) that truly memorable sentence.

Some people take the saying on face value and agree with it. *Well, of course, winning is the only thing. What else would there be?*

Other people are a little uncomfortable with the aggressive little statement. *Well, it's probably true enough in the adult worlds of warfare, business, and sports, but maybe it's not exactly the right message we should be giving to our children at a formative stage in their lives. Let's let them stay innocent for a while longer.*

A third group of people are deeply offended by it. They take it as the distillation of everything that's wrong with football, American culture, capitalism, or mankind. *Well, what else would you expect from the leading pitchman and apologist for a sport that is deeply rooted in ego, greed, and mayhem?*

I think a number of people in this last group have either encountered someone personally, or maybe heard stories about someone they know, who attempted to embody the philosophy that would seem to lie behind the saying. Sometimes I hear these stories myself, about some local Little League coach or Pop Warner coach who has been bashing his kids over the head with some version of "winning isn't everything," And it's not just coaches, I am amazed to see, in my own community, parents pressuring a high school principal to fire a coach who doesn't win enough to suit them.

LOMBARDI RULE #2

Beware the power of quotability.
Pithiness works to the leader's advantage.
But the strong quote out of context can be a distraction.

That's not what my father was about, and that certainly wasn't his leadership model. So what exactly did Vince Lombardi say about winning and results, and what did he mean by it?

THE WILL TO WIN

As I set out to answer this question, I'm much indebted to Michael O'Brien and David Maraniss, the authors of the two best biographies of my father (*Vince* and *When Pride Still Mattered*, respectively). Their having tracked down the colorful origins of the comment gives me more confidence in my analysis of it.

Red Blaik, the legendary head football coach at West Point, was my father's boss, and, by my father's own accounting, the most important influence on his coaching philosophy. Blaik arranged to have hung on the walls of the Army dressing room what he called the "Ten Football Axioms." (This technique of hanging inspirational signs on the locker room walls was imitated by my father in Green Bay.) "The purpose of the game is to win," read one of Blaik's axioms. "To dilute the will to win is to destroy the purpose of the game."

Blaik's wall hangings certainly had a profound effect on my father's psyche. "The will to win" became a stock phrase in The Speech and other of my father's public utterances.

The will to excel and the will to win—they endure.
They are more important than any events that
occasion them.

In his letter of retirement to the Packers' executive committee, Lombardi expanded on the same theme.

Each of us, if we would grow, must be committed
to excellence and to victory; even though we know
complete victory cannot be attained, it must be

pursued with all one's might. The championships,
the money, the color; all of these things linger only
in the memory. It is the spirit, the will to excel, the
will to win; these are the things that endure. These
are the important things, and they will always
remain in Green Bay.

The *will to win* was a constant theme in my father's public comments. And because Lombardi borrowed the phrase from his mentor, Red Blaik, we can almost make the leap to "the purpose of the game is to win" and from there to "winning is the only thing."

IS WINNING EVERYTHING?

Not quite. There is a second and more literal source that we need to blend in here. If you look in a book of quotations, you are likely to find "Winning isn't everything; it's the only thing" attributed to Henry "Red" Sanders, football coach at Vanderbilt University and later at UCLA. Several of Sanders's colleagues at Vanderbilt confirmed that he often recited the saying to motivate his football players in the late 1940s.

Now things take an interesting twist. In 1953, a very forgettable movie called *Trouble Along the Way* was released. It starred John Wayne as a football coach. Wayne played a divorced father who was struggling to win custody of his daughter from his wife. At the same time, he was the type of coach who would do whatever it took to win football games.

Wayne didn't actually utter the famous line himself. That chore was performed by his movie daughter, who claimed to be quoting her father.

But did my father actually pick up the line and use it for his own purposes? Absolutely, although sometimes he tried to hedge the issue. How it got from the silver screen into his head is unclear—I'm not sure he ever saw that particular John Wayne movie—but it definitely was part of his welcoming speech to the players throughout his tenure with the Packers and also during his brief time in Washington. He was even filmed saying it, as part of the welcoming speech that he re-created for the anxious "salesman" who costarred with him in the training film *Second Effort*:

> **Winning isn't everything, but it's the only thing.**
> **In our business, there is no second place.**
> **Either you're first, or you're last.**

He may have guessed that the axiom would raise some hackles, because pretty early on he developed a version that was more appropriate for public consumption. "While winning is not everything, trying to win is everything," he told the American Dairy Association's annual meeting in 1962. Also, "Winning isn't everything, but the desire to win is the only thing," he told *Sports Illustrated's* Tex Maule.

But despite these efforts to put the right spin on things, the quote in its original form slipped out of his control and, to his chagrin, eventually came to define him in the eyes of at least some people. I think that part of the problem was that highly quotable quotes tend to get carved in stone. Part of their appeal is that they're immune to rewrites.

Meanwhile, of course, the times were changing. By the late 1960s, growing numbers of people were questioning whether "victory at all costs" was an ethical, or even a tenable, position. And it's one thing to make a statement in a closed locker room to a few dozen athletes; it's quite another to say the same thing to a national audience.

The criticism of my father began to mount. Combined with some of his other, more colorful comments, it enabled journalists who were so inclined to paint a picture of him as a "take no prisoners" jerk, the kind of guy who might bully Little Leaguers, for example. An *Esquire* article published in the early months of

1968 took this picture to the extreme. It was so negative that it reduced my grandmother—Lombardi's mother—to tears and may have influenced my father's decision to step down as coach in Green Bay.

In this one case at least, Lombardi came to regret his ability to boil down his coaching philosophy to quotable one-liners. Up to a point, it was a good thing to inspire and give direction to your players by keeping the most important guidelines up on the walls, in big letters, just as Red Blaik had done. But past that point, if being quotable led to misunderstandings and controversy, it was clearly counterproductive:

> *I wish to hell I'd never said the damned thing.*
> *I meant the effort . . . . I meant having a goal . . . .*
> *I sure as hell didn't mean for people to crush*
> *human values and morality.*

What lessons should today's leaders take away from this long-ago controversy?

THE EFFORT IS EVERYTHING

First of all, in a very real sense, Lombardi was absolutely right when he told his players, in the privacy of the team meeting room, that *winning was the only thing.* I would make the case that, especially back in his first year or two in Green Bay, he was giving them good career advice. A CEO coming into a turn-around situation would be well advised to consider saying something along the same line, emphasizing results. *This organization is in deep trouble. Either we all produce, or we're all out of here.* And even after the immediate crisis is past, that same CEO might keep reminding people on a regular basis that no organization has a guaranteed right to exist. *Yesterday doesn't matter; we're only winners if we win today.*

LOMBARDI RULE #3

Winning is the only thing—but only in context.
Sometimes the leader has to make the obvious point: If we don't
win, we're out of business. In desperate times, this approach
builds team spirit. In good times, it fights complacency.

In his welcoming speech, Lombardi generally also said something along the lines of the following.

*I'm here because we win. You're here because we
win. When we lose, we're gone.*

A more compelling version of the same idea sometimes followed.

*There are trains, planes, and buses leaving here
every day, and if you don't produce for me, you're
gonna find yourself on one of them.*

At one point, presumably after being publicly scolded once
again for his alleged obsession with winning, my father expressed
his exasperation. "What am I supposed to do, lose?" he complained
aloud to Jim Lawlor, his college roommate from decades earlier.
"They hired me out here to win games."

So in a very real sense, his message to the troops was only a
healthy dose of reality: *Play your heart out and play well, and you
will probably stay with this team. Do anything less, and all bets are
off. Do anything less, and you'd be smart to keep your bags packed.*

And he was also making the obvious point that no matter what
other interests his players had been pursuing in the off-season—business ventures, hobbies, parties—it was now time to get serious again.

*There's not enough thought, not enough dedication
to winning. There's too many outside interests, too*

> *much bow hunting, and all this other*
> *extracurricular what-not.*

There's another ingredient here that anyone who has played competitive sports will agree to adding. Winning is a lot more fun than losing. Football, at least, is not fun. It is hard work and drudgery. The joy is in winning. You only have to contrast the two sidelines at the end of a hard-fought football game to see this point illustrated. Winners get to celebrate, as my father often pointed out; losers only get to grit their teeth and figure out how to win next time.

> *To the winner, there is 100-percent elation,*
> *100-percent fun, 100-percent laughter; and*
> *yet the only thing left to the loser is resolution*
> *and determination.*

So job security and the thrill of victory certainly count for something. But there are still a few more ingredients to add to this picture. Bart Starr, the Packers' quarterback who, along with Jerry Kramer, was probably Lombardi's most perceptive player, once made an interesting comment. "Winning to Lombardi was neither everything nor the only thing," Starr said. "He was more interested in seeing us make the effort to be our best. If we did, he knew that winning would usually take care of itself."

And there's plenty of evidence to suggest that even when the winning didn't "take care of itself," a losing effort that lived up to Lombardi's standards would satisfy the Packers' demanding coach.

Let me give a case in point. On December 9, 1967, the Packers played the Rams in L.A. At that point, the Packers were 9–2–1 on the season and had already clinched the Central Division title. They would soon host the Western Conference title game in Milwaukee, no matter what happened in L.A. From a playoff standpoint, therefore, the game meant very little to the Packers.

Not so for the Rams. They desperately needed a win just to stay in the hunt in what was then called the "Coastal Division." Their record was 9–1–2, but the Baltimore Colts were ahead of them at an even better 10–0–2.

There was rampant speculation in the press that the Packers would take it easy out on the coast. After all, why risk an injury to a starter in a meaningless game? Why not rest the key players? But those who speculated along these lines didn't understand my father. His attitude was, *We are the Green Bay Packers, and we are a proud team.*

By all accounts, the Packers never worked harder in preparation for a game. Even some of the veteran players who knew Lombardi well were surprised at the depth of his determination to win such a seemingly low-stakes game.

The game itself was played with equal intensity. Despite their best efforts, the Packers lost in the final minutes. Jim Murray, the gifted sportswriter for the *Los Angeles Times*, wrote a superb epitaph on the game the next day, witty, warm, and insightful. I think he captured the essence of how my father felt about winning—and *not* winning:

> *When Vince Lombardi loses a football game, particularly with the numbing suddenness that he did that day, it is wise to enter his locker room with a whip and a chair. Not that day. Vince Lombardi's face was suffused with pride. All he had lost was the game. But he hadn't tried to sell the Green Bay Packers with one wheel missing or the engine failing. He hadn't come to town with a plastic team craftily disguised as the real thing. His team lived up to the warranty and no one wanted his money back. No one hollered for the Better Business Bureau.*

I think my father's face would have been suffused with even more pride had the Packers prevailed that day, after making that same heroic effort. And at least in front of friendly groups, my father didn't mind admitting that he liked nothing better than a good win:

> *I used to run the Green Bay Packers. At first, we didn't win. Later on, we won our fair share. Still never as many as I wanted. Which was all of them.*

But the real test here is, was it win at all costs? Or did my father set any limits on himself or his team, even as they set out to win their games?

I think the answer to the first question is clearly no, and the answer to the second is clearly "yes." He did set limits. He was a highly principled man. He never resorted to anything illegal, unethical, or dirty on the playing field. In fact, if any of his players did anything outside the rules, Lombardi would immediately pull them out of the game, whether or not the referees saw the offense or penalized the offender. He liked his football to be played hard and fair. He wanted to win, and win well.

> *Being part of a football team is no different than being a part of any other organization—an army, a political party. The objective is to win, to beat the other guy. You think that is hard or cruel—I don't think it is. I do think it is a reality of life that men are competitive, and the more competitive the business, the more competitive the men. They know the rules, and they know the objective, and they get in the game. And the objective is to win— fairly, squarely, decently, by the rules, but to win.*

Within the rules, he wanted to be *better* than the opponent. "I'm never ready to settle for a tie," he once commented. And even more important, he wanted his players to believe that they were the best in the world. He wanted them to believe that every game was theirs to win:

> *Second place is meaningless. You can't always be first, but you have to believe that you should have been—that you were never beaten—that time just ran out on you.*

We didn't actually lose, he told himself and his players; *we just ran out of time.* It wasn't really a defeat; it was more like a win that was nipped in the bud. *With a little more time, we would have been successful.*

L O M B A R D I   R U L E   # 4

Try to win them all—but play by the rules.
Games are fun only because there are rules and referees. (Football without rules would be an athletic riot. The stock exchange without rules would be an entrepreneurial riot.)

Why this insistence on winning whenever possible and even interpreting losses as wins that were simply frustrated by the clock? I think the answer lies in a phrase my father used frequently: *the winning habit.*

When Lombardi arrived in Green Bay, he found players with the habits and attitudes of mediocrity: Players were painfully aware of their limitations, playing less to win than to avoid embarrassment. In other words, the Packers didn't see themselves as winners. As noted previously, their record the year before he was hired was 1–10–1. Into this difficult situation—a cycle of failure, loss of confidence, and more failure—came Lombardi, a leader and a strong self-believer, with high self-esteem and resiliency. His approach was clear from the outset. *Believe in these players so they can believe in themselves.*

It should be noted that 13 of the players who were part of the 1–10–1 team subsequently went on to be All-Pro.

I've got to make them believers.

That was the first prerequisite for success. The second was the winning habit: the attitudes, skills, and practices that increase one's chances for success. With success would come confidence, which would in turn generate more success. Instead of a vicious cycle, there would be a virtuous circle.

Several years later, one of Lombardi's assistants landed a head coaching job with a team that somewhat resembled the 1958 Packers. He asked my father how he should approach the job. Should he take it easy on the team during the preseason, easing them into a new coaching staff with a different approach? Or should he go flat out, pushing the team from the first day of training camp to transform them into winners? Lombardi's response was unequivocal:

> **There's no question in my mind how you have to approach it. You've got to win every game. Just like we did at Green Bay. Because the guys aren't used to winning. They've never tasted it. They don't know what it's like. You've got to try your damnedest to win every game, no matter what the importance is, because you've got to teach them the winning habit.**

That's the point, I think, *teaching them the winning habit.* Players with winning habits are more likely to win than players with losing habits. Thinking positively about yourself and about your team's prospects improves your chance of success.

GOOD WINNERS, BAD WINNERS

Another way to look at my father's attitude toward winning was to ask what *kind* of winner he was: a good winner, or a bad winner? For example: was he someone who liked to rub other people's noses in the losses he had just handed them?

Here the answer clearly is "no." One reason was purely tactical. He was extremely reluctant to hand a sharp instrument to the other team's coach, to be pulled out of the drawer and used in the next game between the two teams. (A good football coach always has the *next* confrontation between these two teams somewhere in the back of his mind.) He himself loved hanging clips from sportswriters or members of the opposing team on the locker-room walls as motivational spurs for his Packer players. So why wouldn't the other teams use the same ploy? And if they would use it, why should he give them good ammunition unnecessarily?

But beyond these kinds of practical considerations, Vince Lombardi was a *gentleman*. Certain journalists who crossed swords with my father might take issue with this characterization. But as I see it, it's true. And it's just an extension of the point I made earlier: Lombardi was the sort of person who would have hated to spoil a good game, played well by all concerned, with name-calling after the fact.

Again, I can best illustrate the point with a good example. On January 15, 1967, the Packers played the Kansas City Chiefs in the first authentic "super bowl." This game was ballyhooed by the media as a grudge match between the established NFL (as represented by the Packers) and the fledgling AFL. It was the Establishment against the insurgents, the Old Guard versus the Young Upstarts. Some of this was only hype, pumped out there to sell newspapers and push up TV ratings. But some of it was real. There was a lot of bad blood between the leagues. A number of NFL owners told my father that they fully expected the Packers to "uphold the honor of the NFL."

My father, no doubt, felt some animosity toward the AFL. As the Packers' general manager, one of his most important responsibilities was to sign players. The competition from the AFL for good players was complicating his life and also costing his franchise and the rest of the NFL good money. In addition, I'm sure he was tired of hearing about how his Packers were old and tired—a long-in-the-tooth team that had passed its prime—whereas the Chiefs seemed to be the exciting young team of the future.

So emotions were running high that day at the Los Angeles Coliseum. In the minds of the Packers, my father had very deliberately built up the Chiefs as a force to be reckoned with, a serious threat to Packer pride. (The fact was, no one know exactly how good the Chiefs were, since they had never played against any NFL teams.) Not only did the Packers take the threat seriously; I think my father also started to believe his own buildup. He was unusually grumpy at the Friday press conference and was practically jumping out of his skin as game time approached. Frank Gifford, who interviewed him on game day, later said that Lombardi was "shaking like hell." I was there, and I can say that not only was my father as uptight before a game as I had ever seen him, but the tension in the locker room just before game time felt like lightning waiting to be discharged. Once again, for what seemed like the umpteenth time, the pressure was on Vince Lombardi and the Packers to *win*.

And win they did. Although the game stayed close for two quarters, the old veterans from Green Bay ran away with the second half. They wound up winning 35–10, a final score that failed to reflect the true one-sidedness of the contest.

In the postgame press conferences, the journalists in attendance asked Lombardi repeatedly whether the Packers' victory wasn't convincing proof that the NFL was better than the AFL. The same question came at him several times, in several different ways: *So, Coach: Let's call a spade a spade. Aren't you guys in the NFL simply better?* The first few times this bait was dangled in front of my father, he resisted the temptation. Finally, in the excitement of the moment, he forgot his own ground rules about never speaking ill of an opponent. *Yes*, he finally said, *I guess we are better. Are you happy? You got me to say it.*

Coming out of the press conference, he looked pensive, even unhappy. This was not the jubilant coach that his friends, waiting with the car outside the dressing room, expected to see. He explained to a friend what was bugging him:

> **I said something to the press and I wish I could get my words back. I told them that four or five NFL teams could have beaten Kansas City. It was the wrong thing to say, the wrong thing. I came off as an ungracious winner, and it was lousy.**

In other words, even though he was put up to it by the press, he had made an unsportsmanlike mistake. This was out of character; it was not how Lombardi saw himself or wanted others to see him.

LOMBARDI RULE #5

Be a good winner.
This will make your organization proud of itself, and pride will help you in the next round of competition. And anyway, it can't be smart to "diss" the losing side: Won't they just be more motivated next time around?

Lombardi was fond of quoting one of his heroes, General Douglas MacArthur, on the subject of losing well and winning well. "Competitive sports keeps alive in all of us a spirit of vitality and enterprise," MacArthur once wrote, in a paragraph that my father eventually built into The Speech. "It teaches the strong to know when they are weak, and the brave to face themselves when they are afraid. To be proud and unbending in defeat, yet humble and gentle in victory. To master ourselves before we attempt to master others. To learn to laugh, yet never forget how to weep, and it gives a predominance of courage over timidity."

Mastering ourselves before we attempt to master others, being humble and gentle in victory, being a gracious winner—these are certainly not the prescriptions of a win-at-all-costs leader. Winning was critical, but it was neither everything nor the only thing.

HOW TO WIN A FOOTBALL GAME

So far in this book, there hasn't been a lot of worm's-eye-view football. I've used specific game situations to illustrate my points and devoted some space to individual plays (like the Packer Sweep) that reveal something about my father's leadership philosophy. But other than that, I've tried to avoid a lot of details about specific football tactics. If we're in search of the larger themes and lessons of Coach Lombardi's leadership style, then an in-depth consideration of specific blocking patterns or pass routes seems irrelevant.

Some of my father's game plans are stored, carefully, in my office. I think of them as something very special. Football historians and die-hard Packers fans would probably find them as interesting as I do. At the end of the day, though, I think we would agree that all those x's and o's don't reveal a lot about how Lombardi motivated, inspired, and led people.

Even so, I think it would be helpful to take a few of my father's ideas on the specifics of "how to win a football game" and think about their larger implications. Do they, separately or together, tell us more about the Lombardi leadership style? And even after discounting for the fact that football is not business, do they offer us any useful ideas for leading an organization?

*I believe that if you block and tackle better than
the other team and the breaks are even, you're
going to win.*

In other words, put your faith in the fundamentals. "You don't have to have great runners," my father once commented. "You do have to have great blockers." Yes, there's always the chance that the stray fumble or interception will break the game open, either in your favor or against it; but absent that, a good offensive line will win the game for you every time. To me, that sounds like the right prescription for most businesses. Help your front line people, your sales force, your engineers, and the rest is likely to follow.

Every game boils down to doing the things you do best, and doing them over and over again.

So it's fundamentals and it's repetition of the fundamentals, over and over again, without making mistakes, that makes for the win. Again, the parallels to business seem pretty straightforward. Stick to your knitting, as they say in the management literature.

There are only five or six big plays in every game, and you have to make them to win. In a time of crisis, it is absolutely imperative.

LOMBARDI RULE #6

Block and tackle.
Execute the fundamentals, and the rest will follow.

Why stick to fundamentals? Because you never know when the critical moment in the competition is about to happen and because, when that critical moment does arrive, you have to be playing at the top of your game.

I think that this idea has parallels all up and down the line in business. I'm thinking, for example, of issues like product design and engineering, or manufacturing quality control, and so on. Only a consistent standard of excellence will allow you to survive

and prosper. Or, looking at another kind of crisis, when a corporation faces a crisis of public confidence in its products or practices,
such as the Tylenol poisonings back in the 1980s or the Firestone
tire recalls in 2000, the company simply has to be at the top of its
game. It has to think clearly, move quickly and effectively, put out
the fire, and stay in the game.

The team that controls the ball controls the game.

My father made this point in a sales-training film, so we know he
had sales on his mind when he said it. But obviously, ball control
is the name of the game in football. If you hold the ball as long as
you can, you minimize the other team's opportunity to score. The
business corollary is probably something like "Define the turf on
which you choose to compete. Stay on the offensive; don't fall
back to defense. Make your competitors react to you, rather than
the other way around."

There's nothing you can do about
fumbles except scream.

I like this quote. It's partly tongue in cheek. But it reflects the
reality of being a coach on the sidelines on a Sunday afternoon.
Sometimes people are surprised to hear it, but by the time Sunday
rolled around, my father didn't actually have that much to do. The
game plan was in place, and the players were prepared to execute
the plan. Things could go well or badly, but it wasn't as if my father
could run out onto the field and save the day. He was emotional and
demonstrative on the sidelines—he allowed himself a good scream
every now and then—but beyond that, it was up to the players.

Business leaders are in exactly the same position. They are
responsible for defining strategy and tactics, but at the end of the
day, either the people who make up the organization will make that
organization succeed, or they won't.

What my father's quote *doesn't* go on to say, of course, is what would happen in practice the following week, beginning with the Tuesday film session. There, and in subsequent days, my father would find lots of ways to deal with the problem of fumbles and other mistakes. Business leaders certainly have the equivalent, in terms of postmortems, after-action reviews, and changes in policies and practices.

> *You must forget about being cautious, because if you don't you're licked before you start. There is nothing to be afraid of as long as you are aggressive and keep going. Keep going and you will win.*

LOMBARDI RULE #7

Play to jump on opportunity.
If there are only a small number of big plays in the course of a game (or in the life cycle of a product), you have to be playing at a high level of excellence in order to take full advantage of those opportunities.

I put this quote here as a deliberate antidote to several of the preceding ones. Although my father was a believer in the fundamentals and in playing the odds through ball control, he was far from a plodder. He liked a good razzle-dazzle play as much as any coach. The point was to be prepared for all circumstances and act with the confidence that comes from preparation. There were many games in which the Packers faced desperate circumstances—down by more than a field goal with only minutes to play—when Bart Starr marshaled the offense, worked the clock, and aggressively moved the team down the field. They couldn't have done it by being cautious or fearful. They did it by being confident.

Maybe the business equivalent is that the bold departure can be fundamental. In other words, with enough care and preparation, a break from tradition—even a desperation move—can be executed from a position of strength. I've talked to any number of business leaders who tell me that some of their dumbest ideas were turned into winners by people who believed in those ideas and implemented the hell out of them. Be aggressive and keep going!

> *You don't have to win 'em aesthetically.*
> *You win 'em the best you can.*

LOMBARDI RULE #8

Play for elegance, but take any win you can get.
No one comes up with an ugly strategy on purpose.
But sometimes you play on a frozen field or throw into the
wind, and ugly things happen that help you win. Celebrate!

This is an extension of the previous idea, and it speaks to something at the core of my father's philosophy. Good wins aren't always the most elegant ones. Good wins can also be the result of grit, determination, and mental toughness. "Football is a game of inches," Lombardi once said, "and inches make the champion." Even ugly inches count.

The lesson for business? Plan for beauty and elegance as you implement your strategic plan. Assume that you'll beat the competition aesthetically. Then, when you win in some other way—with clumsy or lucky elements, or whatever—celebrate that win just as enthusiastically.

> *You don't win without tradition.*

I think this sounds the theme of "winning habits," but it goes beyond that as well. My father loved to invoke the tradition of "Packer pride," even though before his arrival it had been a very long time since that team had much pride. It's interesting that basketball coach Red Auerbach did much the same thing in Boston, invoking "Celtic pride." If you're playing for something larger than yourself, you're more likely to be an aggressive and successful team player.

Play on tradition.
Tradition motivates. Tradition helps players subordinate their individual interests to the needs of the team.
If you don't have traditions, make some up.

Businesses certainly have their techniques for invoking tradition. Celebrations of significant corporate anniversaries, long-term service pins, lobby displays of product or plant evolutions, brand celebrations, and so on, all designed to help employees feel like they are part of something proud, competent, and competitive, something bigger than themselves.

Using tradition has become more difficult for both sports teams and corporations. It's far less common today for players to spend their entire careers with a single team than it used to be. Similarly, people now leaving college or business school are likely to hold jobs with a half-dozen or more corporations over the course of their working lives. I don't have an answer for this, other than to say that if my father was right—if you don't win without tradition—then organizations have to work doubly hard in today's climate to build and invoke traditions.

A winning coach is simply a guy who finds the winning blend.

Vince Lombardi assembled winning teams the same way mechanical engineers used to design the critical components of automobiles, through the "cut-and-try" approach. The critical difference, of course, is that my father's raw materials were *people*, rather than metals and plastics; and that people change and interact in ways that steel, copper, and petroleum-based products don't. He had to find the winning combination—which, by the way, I don't think he ever thought of as a "simple" task. But again, when the opening kickoff leaves the tee and the clock starts to run, the coach is more or less a spectator. He learns whether he has or has not put together the winning combination.

In business, the winning combination is probably more elusive, in the sense that roles aren't so clearly delineated, there are usually far more players on the field, and hierarchies or divisional structures may get in the way of understanding what's working and not working and why it is or isn't working. Maybe the bottom-line prescription here is a healthy dose of modesty. The leader's role is to set the right play in motion and to more or less get out of the way of the players.

THE PARADOXES OF WINNING

One last general thought on the subject of winning: Getting there may not be all you hoped for.

My father stated one of these paradoxes very succinctly:

> *We want to perfect ourselves so that we can win with less struggle and increasing ease, but the strange thing is that it's not the easy wins we ostensibly seek, but rather the difficult struggles to which we really look forward.*

It's not much fun to play golf in a foursome in which the other three players are far worse than you are. It's equally frustrating to be such a relatively lousy golfer that you slow down the other three members of your foursome. We struggle to improve ourselves to be the *best*. We want to win. But winning isn't the only thing. If we could take a pill to win every contest easily, most of us probably wouldn't take it. As my father would say, the *struggle's* the thing.

The second paradox is probably even more troubling. My father likened success to a narcotic: "It saps the elation of victory," he once said, "and deepens the despair of defeat."

The leader is particularly vulnerable to these highs and lows. The leader is the embodiment of the organization's successes and failures (even though he or she may have less direct impact on those successes and failures than many people in the front lines have). Attempting to explain his reasons for stepping down as the Packers' coach, Lombardi emphasized that a win was sometimes more of a burden than a loss.

> *When I quit, I knew I'd never be back coaching. I knew I wouldn't be able to take it again. The pressures were so horrible. You know, the pressure of losing is bad, awful, because it kills you eventually. But the pressure of winning is worse, infinitely worse, because it keeps on torturing you and torturing you and torturing you. At Green Bay, I was winning one championship after another, after another, after another. I couldn't take it, because I blamed myself, damned myself, whenever they lost a game. I couldn't ever forgive myself for a loss, because I felt I'd let them down. I felt I wouldn't be able to raise myself to the right pitch for the big games, and then I wouldn't be able to raise them to their best effort.*

LOMBARDI RULE #10

Understand the dangers of winning.

If winning comes too hard, your team may get demoralized. But if winning comes too easily, it will be harder to be motivated, even as the world is expecting more and more from you. What's your personal and organizational plan for the day after you succeed?

Obviously, these are the words of a leader in an emotional transition from one phase of his or her life to the next. This leader is reflecting candidly as he or she looks back on a situation that has included both wonderful and difficult elements.

We can't take my father's just-quoted comments at face value. In fact, Lombardi *was* going back to coaching at that very moment, as the newly hired coach of the Washington Redskins. So it's obvious that the lure of being in the game was powerful enough to overwhelm all of the perceived downsides. He had decided that he could reach deep once again and find a way to motivate and inspire himself and his football team.

But it's clear to me, judging from my father's experience, that a leader always has to be looking beyond the next horizon. He or she has to be aware of the old Chinese proverb, *Be careful what you wish for; you may get it.*

He or she has to be asking, constantly, "What happens if, against all these long odds, I *succeed*?"

THE LOMBARDI RULES

Winning

Run to win.
Set a high standard for your team, and keep that standard
out in front (on the wall, on your ring, in your mission statement)
where all can see it.

Beware the power of quotability.
Pithiness works to the leader's advantage. But the strong quote
out of context can be a distraction.

Winning is the only thing—but only in context.
Sometimes the leader has to make the obvious point: If we don't win,
we're out of business. In desperate times, this approach builds team
spirit. In good times, it fights complacency.

Try to win them all—but play by the rules.
Games are fun only because there are rules and referees.
(Football without rules would be an athletic riot. The stock
exchange without rules would be an entrepreneurial riot.)

Be a good winner.
This will make your organization proud of itself, and pride
will help you in the next round of competition. And anyway, it
can't be smart to "diss" the losing side: Won't they just be
more motivated next time around?

Block and tackle.
Execute the fundamentals, and the rest will follow.

Play to jump on opportunity.
If there are only a small number of big plays in the course of a game
(or in the life cycle of a product), you have to be playing at a high level
of excellence in order to take full advantage of those opportunities.

Play for elegance, but take any win you can get.
No one comes up with an ugly strategy on purpose.
But sometimes you play on a frozen field or throw into the wind,
and ugly things happen that help you win. Celebrate!

Play on tradition.

Tradition motivates. Tradition helps players subordinate
their individual interests to the needs of the team.
If you don't have traditions, make some up.

Understand the dangers of winning.

If winning comes too hard, your team may get demoralized.
But if winning comes too easily, it will be harder to be motivated,
even as the world is expecting more and more from you. What's your
personal and organizational plan for the day after you succeed?

"All the Man There Is"

You don't do what is right once in a while, but all of the time.

Maybe this one sentence—all those one-syllable words tumbling out to convey a timeless piece of wisdom—captures the essence of Vince Lombardi's leadership model.

"Of all the lessons I learned from Lombardi," All-Pro guard and author Jerry Kramer once commented, "from all his sermons on commitment and integrity and the work ethic, that one hit home the hardest. I've found in business that only 15 or 20 percent of the people do things right all the time. The other 80 or 85 percent are taking short cuts, looking for the easy way, either stealing from others or cheating themselves. I've got an edge, because whenever I'm tempted to screw off, to cut corners, I hear that raspy voice saying, 'This is the right way to do it. Which way are you going to do it, mister?'"

After my father died, Willie Davis paid a tribute to him that has stuck with me ever since. Davis was the Packers' All-Pro, Hall of Fame defensive end, and he understood my father as well as anybody.

"He is all the man there is," Davis said.

In this short closing chapter, I'd like to make a few final observations about Vince Lombardi, his leadership model, my relationship with him, and his legacy.

A MAN OF PARADOXES

I began this book by describing a man of paradoxes. I'm tempted to end on that same note. Yes, Vince Lombardi could be just as much of an SOB as his biggest detractor ever depicted him. And yes, he could intimidate you if you let him.

And he was a doting grandfather who loved nothing more than getting down on his hands and knees and make silly noises while playing with his grandkids.

LOMBARDI RULE #1

Embrace paradox.
Emerson said it best: *A foolish consistency is the hobgoblin of little minds.*

He could be rude and overbearing toward his players in ways that would take your breath away. Lots of men disliked my father, particularly those who only knew him secondhand, through media reports.

He was also courteous and considerate. Most women were completely charmed by him. They had a lot of difficulty squaring the media image of the terrible Vince Lombardi with this perfect gentleman they had the privilege of meeting.

DEMANDING THE MOST AND THE BEST

As I think the preceding chapters have illustrated, Coach Lombardi was very demanding of his players, his assistants, his family members, and everyone else who came into his orbit. He demanded the *most* they could give and the *best* they could give.

One thing he demanded, probably above all else, was *personal responsibility.* To be "responsible," from my father's perspective, meant being answerable and accountable for your actions and meeting your obligations and duties without prodding from a superior. Around him, you just wouldn't consider dogging it or "mailing it in." That was simply unthinkable.

He held his players to a particularly high standard. They were all gifted athletes who had a responsibility to use their talents to the fullest extent.

> *If you give me anything less than your best, you're*
> *not only cheating yourself, your coaches, your*
> *teammates, everybody in Green Bay, and*
> *everything pro football stands for. You're also*
> *cheating the Maker who gave you the talent.*

"I will try to make each of you the best football player you can possibly be," he told his players time and time again. "I will try with every fiber in me, and I will try and try and try." This wasn't the passion of a coach simply trying to win football games. It was the philosophy of a driven man who felt that all of us have obligations that we can't shirk or avoid.

> *I think a boy with talent has a moral*
> *obligation to use it, and I will not relent*
> *[in] my own responsibility.*

He felt that the truly gifted players had a special obligation in this regard. Every once in a while, a young player with the talent, but not the habits, would arrive in training camp. People knew it was only a matter of time before Vince Lombardi took the new player on as a personal challenge.

> *Talent is not only a blessing; it is a burden,*
> *as the gifted ones will soon find out.*

"When Vin is challenged to try and make a great one out of a ballplayer," my mother Marie once said, "I can only feel sorry for that player. Vin is going to make a hole in his head and pour everything in. When it starts, the player hasn't any idea what he's in for, and he hasn't got a chance. He'll get hammered and hammered and hammered, until he's what Vin wants him to be. You can't resist this thing. You can't fight it."

I don't know how else to live. Unless a man believes in himself, and makes a total commitment to his career, and puts everything he has into it, his mind, his body, and his heart, what's life worth to him?

He also demanded a player's *intelligent effort.* He could excuse physical mistakes, especially if one of his players was matched up against a superior opponent. He could understand a player being blocked out of the play every now and then. As a relatively small college player, after all, he was certainly blocked more than he wanted to be. But it was inexcusable to *stay* blocked.

What Lombardi refused to overlook were mental errors. Mental errors, he insisted, showed a lack of preparation, something within the individual responsibility of each player.

Lombardi's system was simple, logical, and methodical. The players knew what to do, when to do it, and why they did it. He wanted his players to perform free of doubt, and he had a system that was simple enough that he could hold the player accountable for what he did or failed to do.

I have been called a tyrant, but I have also been called the coach of the simplest system in football, and I suppose there is some truth in both of those. The perfect name for the perfect coach would be Simple Simon Legree.

Lombardi also demanded *execution.* If there was a play, you ran it. If there was a rule, you obeyed it. *There would be no excuses.* During practice, he expected every pass to be completed. You'd never point out to him that the ball was wet or the wind was blowing too hard.

He expected his players to adapt to the prevailing conditions. By so doing, he took away a whole universe of excuses.

No excuses.
Help people take responsibility—and then don't accept excuses.

He was equally intolerant of excuses for off-the-field behavior. During his coaching days at St. Cecilia's in New Jersey, he once coached his brother Joe, who was 17 years his junior. Lombardi had a rule that a player had to be in bed by 10 P.M. the night before every game. The big contest for Saints, as for most high school teams, was the Thanksgiving Day game, commonly played against a school's greatest rival. One Thanksgiving eve, Vince's and Joe's mother—my grandmother—asked Joe for help in getting the house ready for the family's Thanksgiving feast, traditionally held after the football game.

Joe agreed and finished cleaning and waxing the floor just after 10 P.M. that night. As he was putting away the pail and mop, Vince walked into the house. He took one look at his younger brother, caught "red-handed" breaking curfew, and said, "You're not playing tomorrow." No matter that young Joe was helping out his mom, who happened to be preparing the dinner that the coach would be eating the next day. No matter that Joe was an All-County guard and a valuable contributor to his team. A rule was a rule. Joe rode bench for the biggest game of the year.

Rigid? Yes. Effective? Yes. Lombardi followed exactly the same procedure on the professional level. During training camp, the Packers had to be in bed—clothes off, lights out—by 11 P.M. One night, Emlen Tunnell, the future Hall of Fame defensive back who played for both the Giants and the Packers, walked into the dorm one minute before 11. There he encountered my father.

"That'll be $50," Lombardi barked.

"Hey," Tunnell objected, surprised. "It's not even 11 yet."

"Yes, Emlen," my father said, in a slightly less stern tone of voice. "But you know you can't be in bed with your clothes off by 11." They both laughed, Tunnell went off to bed—and the fine stuck.

> *Ability involves responsibility; power,*
> *to its last particle, is duty.*

BUILDING ACCOUNTABILITY

If you believe, as I do and as my father did, that leaders don't do much more than make other people more effective at their work, then the leader's most important job is to make people *accountable* for what they do.

Lombardi had a three-pronged approach to building accountability among his players. First, he told his players exactly what he expected of them and why. He believed that they couldn't be held accountable "for" their work if they didn't understand what was expected "of" their work. Almost in a literal sense, he *painted a picture for the players of what it would look like when they performed their job excellently.* During training camp, he would stand at the blackboard and diagram every play that he expected his players to run. He did this for *every player* on every play.

> *You never win a game unless you beat the*
> *guy in front of you. The score on the board*
> *doesn't mean a thing. That's for the fans.*
> *You've got to win the war with the man in*
> *front of you. You've got to get your man.*

But football wasn't simply a collection of individuals "getting their men." Football, my father stressed incessantly, was *teamwork*. Football, at the professional level, was a group of supremely talented athletes making sacrifices for each other, subordinating their individual goals to the goals of the team.

> *"Selflessness," as opposed to "selfishness," is what*
> *I try to teach. "Do your damnedest. Give*
> *everything you've got, because you are playing*
> *with the greatest group, the greatest team, yet to*
> *swing out onto a battlefield." If you can instill that,*
> *you can win ball games.*

The second Lombardi tactic for building accountability was giving the players all the tools they needed to do their jobs. He recognized that he couldn't ask people to take accountability "for" their work if they didn't have everything they needed to "do" their work. Perhaps this sounds self-evident. But look back over the places where you've worked, and ask yourself whether you always had the right tools. Did you ever suffer with an uncomfortable chair, a dumb computer, outmoded software, bad market information, a truck with mechanical ailments, inadequate lighting, or any of the thousand-and-one other problems that plague the typical workplace?

The Packers didn't have these problems or their football equivalents. They had all the tools they needed. They were prepared mentally and physically for every game. They were almost never surprised by what the opposing team did. In the fourth quarter, they almost always found themselves in better physical condition than the opposition. (Their bodies were one of their most important tools.) At my father's insistence, the Packers did everything *first class:* facilities, equipment, travel, and lodging. Lombardi understood that each of these things, considered separately, was more or less trivial. Taken together, though, they created an atmosphere of professionalism. They instilled the clear sense in the minds of the players that everything possible was being done to ensure their success.

Finally, after telling his players what he expected of them and giving them the tools to do it, Lombardi got out of their way. To some extent, the instilling of accountability was a cumulative and continuing process. (Veterans were expected to understand their responsibilities on the first day of training camp; first-year players were cut a little slack until they were brought up to speed.) But there was another dynamic at work as well, a weekly "transfer" of responsibility from coach to team. At the beginning of the week, Lombardi had to break down what had happened on Sunday—both the good and the bad—and point it out to the players. But by midweek, he had to be accentuating the positive and explaining how the Packers were going to win their next game. As I explained in Chapter 6, this was the confidence-building phase.

LOMBARDI RULE #3

Build accountability.
Paint the picture, provide the tools, and get out of the way.

By game time, he knew, the game was out of his hands and in the hands of his players. Of the 70 or so plays in a typical game, Lombardi sent in less than a dozen, and even then, his quarterback had the right to change the play with an audible at the line of scrimmage. It would be an exaggeration to say that the coach was now simply the cheerleader. But in a real sense, the coach was now fan number one of the team he had trained and equipped.

My mother had an interesting perspective on this process. "On Monday, Tuesday, and Wednesday," she used to say half jokingly, "we don't talk, because on Wednesday, he has to go out there and convince himself, the coaches, and the players that they can win. On Thursday, we say hello. On Friday, he is civil." At the beginning of the week, in other words, the weight of the world was on his shoulders. By the end of the week, he had put that weight squarely on the shoulders of the players. He had made them *accountable*.

LOMBARDI ON LOMBARDI, ONE LAST TIME

Being Vince Lombardi's oldest child and only son, bearing the same name and more than a passing physical resemblance to him, has been a mixed bag. The thrill and excitement of being around pro football, the championships, the opportunity to rub shoulders with (and even become friends with) some of the greatest football players of that era—these are experiences I wouldn't trade for anything.

Being a teenager whose father was the most famous sports personality of his day was another matter. It seemed like there was always *pressure*. Some of the pressure was imposed from the outside; lots more of it was self-imposed. For example, how do you handle the simple act of meeting someone? Do you give them a confident handshake and say, in a firm voice, "Hi, I'm Vince Lombardi!" If you do, isn't it likely they're going to think you're a little too full of yourself, riding on Dad's coattails?

Or do you try to fade into the woodwork? Do you mumble your name during the introductions, hoping no one will make the connection?

And what happens when they *do* make the connection? What do you do when, in their eyes, you see the unspoken assessment: *Well, he's nothing like his father.*

For much of my life, I opted to stay in the background. Far too late, I realized that that was a mistake. I realized that what other people think and feel is their problem. Maybe I can influence it; maybe I can't.

Today, I'm very comfortable with who my father was and who I am. The fact that I'm a professional speaker and that I've written a book about my father's leadership model is a reflection of that comfort. Writing this book and speaking to groups around the country gives me an opportunity to celebrate my father's accomplishments, to interpret him for new and younger audiences, and to add my own reflections on leadership as they evolve over time. It's a rewarding life, and I'm grateful to my father for the part he played in it.

You can't just dream yourself into character.
You must hammer— you must forge—one
out for yourself.

Sam Huff, the great middle linebacker for the Giants and Redskins who also served as a Redskin coach under Lombardi, once recalled a conversation he had with my father. Lombardi was excited because he thought that he was in a position to leave his family an inheritance of a million dollars. That was a lot of money, in 1968 dollars, and it was quite an accomplishment for the butcher's son from New York.

Huff was bold enough to contradict him—or at least, to suggest a different way of looking at things. "Coach," he said, "you've already given your family something that's worth a whole lot more than any money you could ever leave. You've given them the Lombardi name."

LOMBARDI RULE #4

Treasure your legacy.
Appreciate what's been given to you.
Give as much to someone else.

I don't know how my father reacted to that comment. But from my perspective, Sam got it right.

After the cheers have died down and the stadium is
empty, after the headlines have been written, and
after you are back in the quiet of your room and
the championship ring has been placed on the
dresser and all the pomp and fanfare have faded,
the enduring thing that is left is the dedication to
doing with our lives the very best we can to make
the world a better place in which to live.

THE LOMBARDI RULES

All the man there is

Embrace paradox.
Emerson said it best: *A foolish consistency is the hobgoblin of little minds.*

No excuses.
Help people take responsibility—and then don't accept excuses.

Build accountability.
Paint the picture, provide the tools, and get out of the way.

Treasure your legacy.
Appreciate what's been given to you. Give as much to someone else.

Endnotes

CHAPTER 1

I've been in football... From Vince Lombardi's "Dayton" speech, 6/22/70.

At many a moment... O'Brien, Michael. *Vince.* William Morrow and Company, Inc. New York: 1987, p. 200.

The Good Lord gave... Wiebusch, John (editor). *Lombardi.* A National Football League Book, distributed in 1971 by Follett Publishing Co., Chicago, p. 55.

Before I can embrace freedom... From a Vince Lombardi interview with the Newspaper Enterprise Association in Vince Lombardi, Jr.'s collection, undated, conducted by Murray Olderman.

I tend to believe... Briggs, Jennifer. *Strive to Excel.* Rutledge Hill Press. Nashville: 1997, p. 114.

Don't succumb to excuses... From an undated Vince Lombardi talk, "Goal Posts," in Vince Lombardi, Jr.'s collection.

Brains without competitive hearts are rudderless. From Vince Lombardi's 9/2/65 talk honoring St. Norbert's Father Burke, in Vince Lombardi, Jr.'s collection.

You can call me a dictator. These are from an article by Bob Oates, (Times Staff Writer), entitled "The Lombardi Method: Analyze the Talent." Undated, unattributed photocopy supplied by Vince Lombardi, Jr. From the time period when he took over the Redskins.

A meeting is only... From Vince Lombardi's 4/27/60 meeting with the Wisconsin chapter of the Public Relations Society of America, in Vince Lombardi, Jr.'s collection.

In order to succeed... From a speech in Vince Lombardi, Jr.'s collection.

We're going to have a winner... Johnson, William, "Arararaararararrargh!" *Sports Illustrated*, pp. 28–33, quoted at a press conference.

"He was widely known as St. Vincent." *ibid.*

"Gentlemen," he began... *ibid.*

"Vince Lombardi Day..." George, Gary (editor). *Winning is a Habit*. Harper Collins Publishers, Inc. New York: 1997, p. 140.

"Nobody wants to be a legend, really... *Sports Illustrated*. Also cited in Dowling, Tom. *Coach: A Season with Lombardi*. W.W. Norton & Company, Inc. New York: 1970, p. 316.

"Lombardi remembered all the breaks..." *Lombardi*, p. 91.

"In pro football," he... *Lombardi*, p. 48.

"Lombardi," Blaik said... *Coach*, p. 15.

"He is volatile, and of a temper..." From Earl H. Blaik's (EHB) introduction of Vince Lombardi, guest of honor, at a dinner held in NYC in May 1966, when Fordham gave Vince Lombardi its "Insignis Medal." Supplied to Vince Lombardi by EHB in letter dated 2/28/67. Blaik's remarks were forwarded to Vince Lombardi by EHB on 2/28/67; now in Vince Lombardi, Jr.'s collection.

CHAPTER 2

One of our goals in life... From an undated Vince Lombardi talk entitled "Goal Posts," in Vince Lombardi, Jr.'s collection.

If I had to... Briggs, Jennifer. *Strive to Excel*. Rutledge Hill Press. Nashville: 1997, p. 64

"He can be the way he is ..." *Coach*, p. 208.

No leader, however great... George, Gary (editor). *Winning is a Habit*. Harper Collins Publishers, Inc. New York: 1997, p. 67; also Vince Lombardi's 12/5/68 speech to the 73rd Congress of American Industry, sponsored by the National Association of Manufacturers;

other versions in other speeches, including the 6/22/70 "Dayton" speech.

There is something in great men... From Vince Lombardi's 6/22/70 "Dayton" speech.

The difference [between a good... Lombardi, Vince. *Run to Daylight.* Simon & Schuster Inc. New York: 1963, p. 19.

CHAPTER 3

The value of all our daily... Briggs, Jennifer. *Strive to Excel.* Rutledge Hill Press. Nashville: 1997, p. 88; also Vince Lombardi's 6/22/70 Dayton, OH, "Final Speech."

I gave it some thought. First appeared in the 9/70 issue of *The Washingtonian.*

Every little knowledge... From an undated Vince Lombardi talk entitled "Goal Posts," in Vince Lombardi, Jr.'s collection.

A team expresses... Run to Daylight, p. 113.

"The successful man is himself..." First half of quote is from *Strive to Excel*, p. 66; second half is from Vince Lombardi's 6/22/70 "Dayton" speech.

In all my years... Run to Daylight, p. 113.

When we place our... From Vince Lombardi's 5/64 speech to the First Friday Club of Los Angeles, in Vince Lombardi's collection.

Adversity is the... Strive to Excel, p. 94.

I believe I wanted... Run to Daylight, p. 101.

It was absolutely... Sports Illustrated.

I'm not an overly modest man. Sports Illustrated.

CHAPTER 4

The great hope... Strive to Excel, p. 61, but basically the tag line to all his speeches.

Character is the... Vince Lombardi's speech to the NAM, 12/15/68, in Vince Lombardi, Jr.'s collection.

I never tell... Sports Illustrated.

While statistics are... *Run to Daylight*, p. 78.

Keep in mind that... From undated Vince Lombardi talk entitled "Goal Posts," in Vince Lombardi, Jr.'s collection.

The ego destroys... From a speech delivered by Vince Lombardi at the Fathers-Sons Communion Brunch at St. Bonaventure Prep, Sturtevant, Wisconsin, 4/16/67, but also in Vince Lombardi's 5/64 speech to the First Friday Club in Los Angeles.

Whatever the reasons... *Winning is a Habit*, p. 134.

If I ever hear... Maraniss, David. *When Pride Still Mattered*. Simon & Schuster, Inc. New York: 1999, p. 241.

I'll never—absolutely never... *Vince*, p. 266.

If you're black or white... *Vince*, p. 265.

"Why," he asked his golfing buddies... *Winning is a Habit*, p. 242.

Every year I try... *Strive to Excel*, p. 53; *Vince*, p. 262.

CHAPTER 5

Work and sacrifice... *Strive to Excel*, p. 134; Vince Lombardi's 6/22/70 "Dayton" speech.

Improvements in moral... From an undated Vince Lombardi talk entitled "Goal Posts," in Vince Lombardi, Jr.'s collection.

Hell, I'm an emotional man. Sports Illustrated.

There's nothing personal... *Strive to Excel*, p. 96; quoted from *Second Effort*, a sales-training film produced by the Dartnell Corporation, Chicago.

Once you agree... *Strive to Excel*, p. 95.

Every vocation calls... From an undated Vince Lombardi talk entitled "Goal Posts," in Vince Lombardi, Jr.'s collection.

"When I speak of 'Spartanism...'" This version is from a speech delivered by Vince Lombardi at the Fathers-Sons Communion Brunch at St. Bonaventure Prep, Sturtevant, Wisconsin, 4/16/67, but there's a close approximation in The Speech, the 6/22/70 "Dayton" speech, and others.

The only way I know... *Run to Daylight*, p. 24.

"Everything with him is..." *Coach*, p. 329.

A guy may have... From a 6/29/70 Vince Lombardi speech, "What Makes It Great?"

"When the other coaches..." *Lombardi*, p. 71.

I believe a man... Sports Illustrated.

"Dear Tim..." *Lombardi*, p. 15.

"I can't put my finger..." *When Pride Still Mattered*, p. 63.

Mental toughness is... Strive to Excel, p. 108.

CHAPTER 6

Most people in business... From Vince Lombardi's 12/5/68 speech to the 73rd Congress of American Industry, sponsored by the NAM.

In dealing with... Strive to Excel, p. 17.

How does one achieve... From Vince Lombardi's 12/5/68 speech to the 73rd Congress of American Industry, sponsored by the NAM.

"That means a lot." *Strive to Excel*, p. 129.

The objective is to win... Strive to Excel, p. 40.

Each of us must... From Vince Lombardi's 6/22/70 "Dayton" speech (also in *Strive to Excel*, p. 60, in partial form).

Morally, the life... From Vince Lombardi's 4/27/60 meeting with the Wisconsin chapter of the Public Relations Society of America.

"We've got the young radicals..." From a Vince Lombardi interview with the Newspaper Enterprise Association, undated, in Vince Lombardi, Jr.'s collection, conducted by Murray Olderman.

"You hear the expression that this is the 'now generation...'" "The Lombardi Method."

"The guy had such..." *Lombardi*, p. 72.

"It was amazing..." *Lombardi*, p. 45.

A leader is judged... Strive to Excel, p. 19.

"Will you pray..." *Vince*, p. 140.

"The man who is trained..." *Second Effort.*

We are going to win some games. Strive to Excel, p. 30.

To play with confidence... Run to Daylight, p. 189.

As soon as error... Strive to Excel, p. 89.

"The whole psychology..." *Vince*, p. 151.

"You'd be surprised…" *Second Effort.*

"That's a human constant…" *Coach*, p. 312.

If you settle for… Strive to Excel, p. 37.

"Your consistent unwillingness…" From an undated letter from Starr to Vince Lombardi, in Vince Lombardi, Jr.'s collection.

"The satisfactions are few…" *Run to Daylight*, p. 47.

The closer you get … Coach, p. 274.

What is defeat? Strive to Excel, p. 99.

"That is the measure…: *Winning is a Habit*, p. 35.

"You never find… "The Lombardi Method."

"When we lost…" *Second Effort.*

"He refuses to accept defeat…" *Coach*, p. 288.

To be the coach of… From a 6/29/70 Vince Lombardi speech, "What Makes It Great?"

"I never tell a player…" "The Lombardi Method."

"Vin was a great teacher…" *When Pride Still Mattered*, pp. 161–162.

They call it coaching… Run to Daylight, p. 101.

"I loved the meetings." *When Pride Still Mattered*, p. 213.

"He was a great teacher…" *Vince*, p. 350.

"You've got to live it all day long…" *Coach*, p. 330.

Coaching is selling… Second Effort.

"Lombardi is a salesman…" *Coach*, p. 130.

Leaders are lonely people … Strive to Excel, p. 19.

There's a great closeness … Sports Illustrated.

CHAPTER 7

You know why football is so popular? Coach, p. 321.

"I guess it was inevitable…" *Strive to Excel*, p. 44.

"They were fussing…" *Lombardi*, p. 70.

There aren't any owners... *Vince*, p. 212.

It had to be autonomy... *Sports Illustrated*.

I want it understood... *Vince*, p. 139.

If I were coaching... *Coach*, p. 31; *Vince*, p. 326.

You mean, a one-man operation... *Coach*, p. 275.

Rozelle later said that... *Vince*, p. 200.

You gotta remember one thing... *Lombardi*, p. 193.

I think I'd be unhappy... *When Pride Still Mattered*, p. 275.

"He knew where every paper clip was..." *Lombardi*, p. 91.

As an example, Burns recalls... *Lombardi*, p. 136.

That was the last question... *Lombardi*, p. 85.

"It is unwise..." "The Lombardi Method."

The two main things... "The Lombardi Method."

For a whole half season... *Run to Daylight*, p. 67.

We put tremendous pressure... From a 6/29/70 Vince Lombardi speech, "What Makes It Great?"

I'm going to ask you... *Second Effort*.

Good physical condition... *Second Effort*.

"Lombardi works you so hard..." *Run to Daylight*, p. 171.

The harder you work... *Strive to Excel*, p. 30.

"Maybe that's the key..." Coach, p. 218.

I don't want any... *Lombardi*, p. 48.

"Lombardi explained that some..." *Strive to Excel*, p. 54.

"The one [play] everybody..." *Run to Daylight*, p. 12.

There's nothing spectacular... *Run to Daylight*, p. 97.

One must not hesitate... *Strive to Excel*, p. 21.

What it will all come... *Run to Daylight*, p. 112.

The element of surprise... Run to Daylight, p. 112.

"If you can be traded..." *Coach*, p. 285.

A professional football team... Run to Daylight, p. 55.

CHAPTER 8

Conquests are won... From Vince Lombardi's 6/22/70 "Dayton" speech.

This is not easy... Run to Daylight, p. 88.

It's no damn fun... Coach, p. 314.

I am going to find... Vince, p. 143.

I'm just going to... Vince, p. 249.

"All *right*," barked my father... Plimpton, George. *One More July.* Harper & Row: New York, 1977, pp. 24–26.

Perhaps you didn't realize... When Pride Still Mattered, p. 265.

There is a time... Strive to Excel, p. 24.

"What was that all about..." *When Pride Still Mattered*, p. 394.

"It took the edge off the tension..." *Vince*, p. 245.

"The truth is," halfback Donny Anderson. From an unidentified newsclip in Vince Lombardi, Jr.'s files.

You can't coach ... "The Lombardi Method."

[Jordan] has a tendency... Run to Daylight, p. 70.

"I walked into his office..." *Lombardi*, p. 180.

"It's the motivation that's the thing..." *Lombardi*, p. 171.

I hold it more important... Winning is a Habit, p. 106.

"When I think of him..." *Vince*, p. 351.

There are some people... Coach, p. 314.

Changes take time... From an undated Vince Lombardi talk entitled "Goal Posts," in Vince Lombardi Jr.'s collection.

The achievements of an... Strive to Excel, p. 83.

"He was tough and abusive..." *Vince*, p. 247.

"The shoutings, encouragements..." From an undated letter in Vince Lombardi, Jr.'s collection from Starr to Vince Lombardi.

CHAPTER 9

The will to excel... From Vince Lombardi's 12/5/68 speech to the 73rd Congress of American Industry, sponsored by the NAM.

Each of us, if we... When Pride Still Mattered, p. 458.

"Winning isn't everything..." From a Vince Lombardi speech upon accepting the chairmanship for the 1962 Wisconsin Dairy Month, and from a "The View From Here" column; both in Vince Lombardi, Jr.'s collection.

I wish to hell I'd... Winning is a Habit, p. 15; *Vince*, p. 197 (quoting a conversation with sportswriter Jerry Izenberg).

I'm here because we win. Winning is a Habit, p. 12.

"They hired me out..." *Vince*, p. 197.

There's not enough thought... Strive to Excel, p. 135..

To the winner, there is... Vince Lombardi's 6/22/70 final speech in Dayton, OH, in Vince Lombardi, Jr.'s collection.

"He was more interested in..." *Strive to Excel*, p. 116.

I used to run the Green Bay Packers. From a 6/29/70 Vince Lombardi speech, "What Makes It Great?"

Being part of a football... Strive to Excel, p. 40.

"I'm never ready to..." *Lombardi*, p. 11.

Second place is meaningless. Strive to Excel, p. 27.

There's no question... Lombardi, p. 87.

I said something... Lombardi, p. 139.

"It teaches the strong..." Original source unknown, but quoted constantly in Vince Lombardi's speeches (e.g., his speech to the National Association of Manufacturers, 12/15/68).

I believe that if... Run to Daylight, p. 47.

"You don't have to... From Martin F. Nolan's 2/7/69 *Boston Globe* column, inserted in the *Congressional Record* by Representative Robert O. Tiernan.

Every game boils down... Run to Daylight, p. 49.

There are only... Winning is a Habit, p. 13.

The team that controls... Second Effort.

There's nothing you can do... Run to Daylight, p. 78.

You must forget about... Strive to Excel, p. 135.

You don't have to... Winning is a Habit, p. 8.

You don't win... From a speech delivered by Vince Lombardi at the Fathers-Sons Communion Brunch at St. Bonaventure Prep, Sturtevant, Wisconsin, 4/16/67.

A winning coach is... "The Lombardi Method."

We want to perfect ourselves... Run to Daylight, p. 20; *Vince*, p. 201.

"It saps the elation..." *Lombardi*, p. 87.

When I quit, I knew I'd... Sports Illustrated.

EPILOGUE

You don't do what is... Strive to Excel, p. 61.

'This is the right..." *Vince*, p. 383.

You never win a game... Lombardi, p. 59.

"Selflessness," as opposed to... From a 6/29/70 Vince Lombardi speech, "What Makes It Great?," in Vince Lombardi, Jr.'s collection.

You can't just dream... From a speech delivered by Vince Lombardi at the Fathers-Sons Communion Brunch at St. Bonaventure Prep, Sturtevant, Wisconsin, 4/16/67.

Index

To view and order

What It Takes To Be #1

Please go to www.vincejr.com